A WALKING TOUR

Sketches of the city'

Journey through Bangkok's urban landscape

Gregory Byrne Bracken

Marshall Cavendish
Editions

All text and illustrations by G. Byrne Bracken
Editor: Cheryl Sim
Designer: Benson Tan

© 2010 Marshall Cavendish International (Asia) Private Limited

Published by Marshall Cavendish Editons
An imprint of Marshall Cavendish International
Times Centre, 1 New Industrial Road, Singapore 536196
Tel: (65) 6213 9300   Fax: (65) 6285 4871
E-mail: genref@sg.marshallcavendish.com
Online Bookstore: www.marshallcavendish.com/genref

Other Marshall Cavendish offices
Marshall Cavendish Ltd. PO Box 65829, London EC1P 1NY, UK · Marshall Cavendish
Corporation. 99 White Plains Road, Tarrytown NY 10591-9001, USA · Marshall
Cavendish International (Thailand) Co Ltd. 253 Asoke, 12th Flr, Sukhumvit 21 Road,
Klongtoey Nua, Wattana, Bangkok 10110, Thailand · Marshall Cavendish (Malaysia)
Sdn Bhd, Times Subang, Lot 46, Subang Hi-Tech Industrial Park, Batu Tiga, 40000
Shah Alam, Selangor Darul Ehsan, Malaysia

Marshall Cavendish is a trademark of Times Publishing Limited

National Library Board (Singapore) Cataloguing in Publication Data
Byrne Bracken, G. (Gregory)
Bangkok : a walking tour / Gregory Byrne Bracken. – Singapore :
Marshall Cavendish Editions, c2010.
p. cm.
Includes index.
ISBN-13 : 978-981-4302-22-7 (pbk.)

1. Walking – Thailand – Bangkok – Guidebooks. 2. Historic buildings – Thailand –
Bangkok – Guidebooks. 3. Historic sites – Thailand – Bangkok – Guidebooks.
4. Bangkok (Thailand) – Tours. 5. Bangkok (Thailand) – Guidebooks. I. Title.

DS589.B2
915.93—dc22   OCN646213057

Printed in Singapore by Times Printers Pte Ltd

Dedicated to the memory of my aunt and uncle,
Marian and Charles Byrne.

CONTENTS

Acknowledgments

This is just to thank all those who have helped me with this book, particularly Cheryl Sim, who has been such an excellent editor, Benson Tan for the lovely art direction, Melvin Neo for his support throughout the entire 'Walking Tour' series. Darren Ying, for always helping me with my Chinese translations. And finally, and most importantly, Robert Cortlever, the man who first introduced me to this fascinating city and who has enriched my life ever since.

SUGGESTED ITINERARIES

History
Charoen Krung Road
Rattanakosin
Bang Lamphoo
Dusit District

Culture
Rattanakosin
Dusit District
Further Afield

Markets
Prathunam
Silom Road
Charoen Krung Road
Chinatown
Bang Lamphoo
Further Afield (Chatuchak Weekend Market)

Shopping
Prathunam
Wireless Road
Silom Road
Charoen Krung Road
Chinatown

Children's
Prathunam
Dusit District

Introduction

Bangkok is notorious for its traffic, which means that walking is one of the best ways of getting around the city. It is also greener than most people realise with a number of different areas, almost cities within a city, which are best explored on foot.

Each chapter of this book shows a suggested walking route, each following on from where the previous one left off. These try to cover one particular area per walk, like Chinatown or Rattanakosin, but the city's Downtown is so large that it has been split into three separate walks. Distances can be huge, city blocks in Bangkok are big and have few crossing streets, the advantage is that once you're on the road you'll have less chance of missing the things you want to see. The buildings and sites listed are only suggestions for visiting, they don't have to be followed rigorously, and apart from the usual temples, mosques, churches and museums there's also information on other places of interest, like skyscrapers which have restaurants, bars or galleries with good views of the city.

Be careful when following some of the routes as Bangkok can be treacherous — uneven paving, crumbling edges, even gaping holes that are left unprotected — so watch your step, particularly when you have your eyes gazing upward at the buildings. Remember to stop often, don't overdo it in the tropical weather. Drink plenty of liquids, and there are numerous shops, cafes and restaurants en route to stop in and rest. Parts of Bangkok can be surprisingly green, with shady trees lining the roadways, but increasingly shadows seem to be coming from the increasingly tall buildings in and around the city.

Most of Bangkok's streets are lively day and night, and there's nearly always something interesting to see, and smell or even taste, so enjoy the experience. Do remember, however, that if you want to go into places like temples and some museums you must dress appropriately (i.e. you can't wear shorts, tee-shirts or sandals).

Monk and friend

Notes

A Note on History

After a particularly savage attack by the Burmese in 1767, Auytthaya, the capital of Siam (as the Kingdom of Thailand was then known), was destroyed. It had been the country's capital for more than four centuries and had been as large and rich as many European cities. The site was now considered too vulnerable and so a new capital was founded by King Taksin farther down the Menam River at Thonburi. A short time later the King went mad and was overthrown by one of his generals, Phraya Chakri, who put him to death. Phraya Chakri then took the title Rama I and founded the Chakri dynasty, which still reigns today, King Bumibol (pronounced Bumibon) is known as Rama IX.

> **Did You Know?**
> King Taksin was executed in the prescribed way for Thai royalty, by being tied up in a velvet sack and beaten to death with a sandalwood club.

Rama I then moved the capital, which was known to Westerners as Bancok, or the village of the wild plum, to the more easily defended eastern side of the river, forcing the Chinese merchants who had settled there to move farther downstream to what is present-day Chinatown. He built a series of defensive canals, a palace and a new temple to house the Emerald Buddha. He called the new 'Royal Island' Rattanakosin, but the name Bangkok stuck in Westerners' minds. At Rama I's coronation in 1782 he renamed the new capital Khrung Thep Phra Maha Nakhorn (the City of Angels, the Capital City), and it is still known to Thais as Khrung Thep (City of Angels) a shortened form of what has since become the longest city name in the world.

Until the second half of the twentieth century the main means of transport in the city was by boat, and though a lot of the canals, known as *khlongs*, have since been culverted, it still remains one of the best ways to see Bangkok. Filling in the canals wasn't just an aesthetic impoverishment, the waterways had acted as drains for the entire delta and their loss has left the city more prone to flooding than ever, but it didn't do enough to alleviate the road shortage anyway. The Chao Phraya River, which changed its name from the Menam in honour of Rama I, is teeming with craft, from huge cargo barges to ferries and longtail boats, and is the backbone of a network of canals, which in Thonburi are still relatively intact and give a flavour of what Bangkok life used to be like

Towards the end of the nineteenth century, Rama V relocated the royal family to the Dusit district in the north of the city, where he constructed impressive avenues, palaces and temples, while the area around Sathorn

Map of Thailand

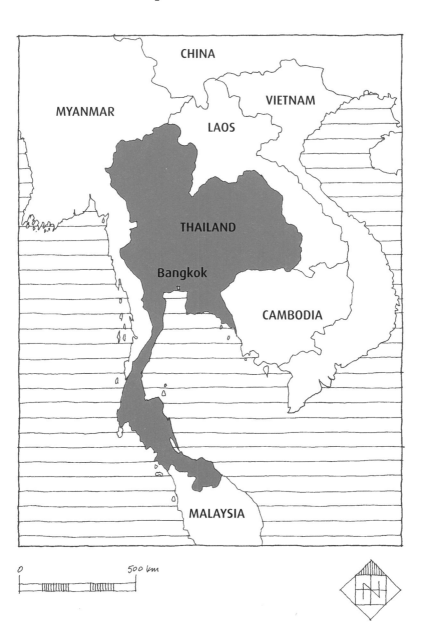

and Silom Roads became a fashionable enclave for rich foreigners who built gracious villas overlooking the wide roads and tree-lined canals.

The second half of the twentieth century saw uncontrolled urban expansion, particularly to the east. Bangkok in 1900 was about 13 square kilometres, but by 1980 had ballooned to 330 square kilometres, and it is still growing. Earlier attempts at orderly planning were obliterated and the city now has a series of different centres; from Rattanakosin and Chinatown, to the area between Silom Road and Prathunam, and even Sukhumvit Road. But if the visitor is prepared to explore, the city can be very rewarding, with pockets of charm in the oddest places, from serene temples, to lush parks, and even little corners of traditional activity that still take place much as they must have done in the days of Rama I.

Note: Siam

When Field Marshall Phibul became Prime Minister of Siam in 1939 he changed the name to Muang Thai (Land of the Thai), even though it is more commonly called Prathet Thai (Kingdom of the Thai) by the Thais themselves, and almost exclusively Thailand, an odd mix of Thai and English, by the rest of the world. It was done partly to try and break the Chinese stranglehold on the Thai economy (the overseas Chinese here are less visible than in other Southeast Asian countries, but their influence is still considerable), and to lay claim to territory housing Thai people which had been lost to the neighbouring French and British colonial empires over the previous decades. By allying themselves with Japan during World War II Thailand hoped to regain what had been unjustly wrested from them, in this they were unsuccessful, but like other politically motivated name changes, Ceylon (Sri Lanka), Irian Jaya (New Guinea), Burmah (Myanmar), Siam has perhaps lost something in the translation.

A Note on Climate

Bangkok's climate is governed by three seasons: the cool season, running from November to February, is the pleasantest time to visit, temperatures average around 27 degrees; the hot season, beginning in March, with highs of up to 37 degrees; and the rainy season, which varies from year to year, but usually starts in May and reaches a climax in September or October, with eighty per cent of the annual rainfall occurring during the late afternoon showers, which are often accompanied by spectacular thunder and lightning.

A Note on Spelling

Spellings differ in Bangkok, on maps, in guides and even from place to place. Those in this guide are standardised with a mind to simple, clear pronunciation.

Bangkok Districts

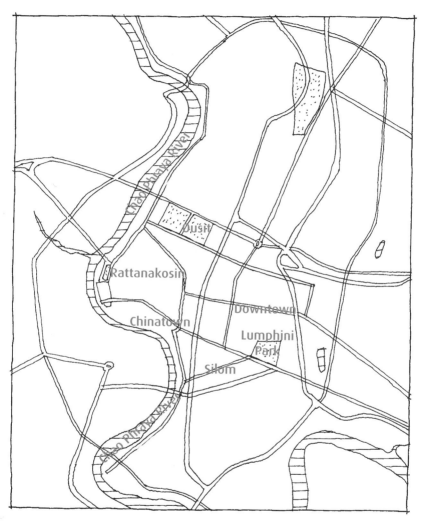

Chao Phraya River

Dusit

Rattanakosin

Chinatown

Downtown

Lumphini Park

Silom

Chao Phraya River

0   5 km

A Note on Icons

To inform readers about the interesting features of the places they pass, we have added icons, drawn by the author, to represent the following:

 Must See

 National Monument

 Good View

 See At Night

 Drinking

 Eating

 Shopping

A Note on Dress

You should dress comfortably for the tropics, but remember that in Thailand you should also cover up your body as much as possible. You will not be allowed into places such as temples wearing short trousers or short-sleeved shirts. Shoes must be removed before entering certain buildings, temples mainly, but some homes and offices will expect you to do so as well, basically if you see a pile of shoes at or near an entrance, you should remove your own as well before entering.

Note on Social Behaviour

Thais address people by their first name, usually with the word '*khun*' in front of it, which is used for both males and females. Thais rarely shake hands, using the traditional form of greeting known as the '*wai*' to say hello, goodbye, thank you and to apologise. As complex in its social ramifications as the Japanese bow, the *wai* is a prayer-like gesture made with palms pressed together in front of the chest, nose or forehead. Feel free to imitate one if someone *wais* to you — any clumsiness will be forgiven — but it's best not to initiate one as it can be embarrassing, particularly for the Thais. Never raise your voice or allow yourself to seem angry, you'll be even less likely to achieve your objectives — Thais avoid confrontation at all costs. Pointing your feet at anyone is considered rude, so be careful how you sit, especially if you're crossing your legs, never put your feet on a table. In temples, make sure you sit with your feet tucked away from the sacred images. Public displays of physical affection, other than innocent ones between friends such as hand-holding, are generally frowned upon.

A Note on Taboos
Monks are revered in Thailand, and most Thai men spend at least some part of their lives in a monastery. Most taboos to do with monks concern women, who are not allowed to touch a monk, or directly hand anything to one. The royal family is not only revered but is genuinely loved. Criticising or defaming them will not only be crass and offensive, but can, under certain circumstances, be considered a crime. Because the Thai currency bears the king's image, you must treat it with respect, and if you happen to be anywhere and they start to play the National Anthem, follow the lead of the Thais around you and stand to attention.

Checklist

Sunglasses.
Sunscreen.
A small umbrella for the frequent showers. It can also come in useful as a parasol.
A small hand towel.
A small bottle of something to drink is essential.
Tiger Balm, when applied promptly to mosquito bites is extremely effective in preventing them from itching and becoming inflamed.

"Bangkok is the most hokum place I have ever seen, never having been to California. It is a triumph of the 'imitation' school; nothing is what it looks like; if it is not parodying European buildings it is parodying Khmer ones; failing anything else it will parody itself."

— Geoffrey Gorer, *Bali and Angkor*

Prathunam

Downtown North

Prathunam means 'water gate' in Thai and refers to the canal lock which used to be located on Khlong San Sap here. This area is home to an interesting mix of buildings, old and new, including the prestigious Chulalongkorn University, Jim Thompson's famous Thai-style house, as well as Baiyoke Tower II, the tallest building in the country.

THE WALK

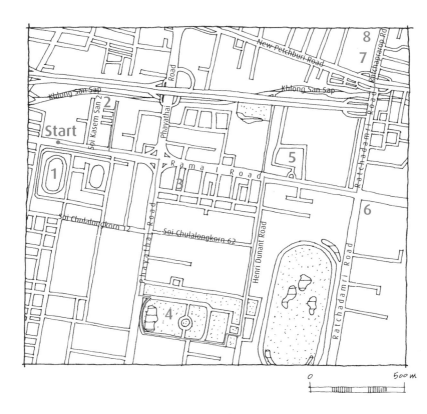

KEY

1. National Stadium
2. Jim Thompson's House
3. Siam Square
4. Chulalongkorn University
5. Wat Pathum Wanaram
6. Erawan Shrine
7. Prathunam Market
8. Baiyoke Tower II

Prathunam

National Stadium

National Stadium

If you are walking from the National Stadium Skytrain Station, follow Rama I Rd away from the direction of Phayathai Rd and the National Stadium will be the first building you see on your left. Also known as Prathunam Stadium, this is Thailand's main arena for soccer and other sporting events. Thais are enthusiastic followers of soccer, especially the English Premier League, and a professional football league was started in 1996. The white, stylised art deco frontage of the stadium is quite elegant and on closer look, incorporates some interesting Thai motifs.

Jim Thompson's House

With the National Stadium on your right, walk along Rama I Rd and turn left into Soi Kasem San 2. Jim Thompson's House will be on your left at the end of this narrow laneway. Thompson was instrumental in reviving the Thai silk industry after World War II, and in 1959 built his own home from a number of traditional Thai houses which he brought down to Bangkok from Ban Khrua and Ayutthaya. These were then reassembled in an unconventional layout, with some of the walls even turned inside out to better highlight their craftsmanship.

The small garden is densely planted and overlooks a narrow stretch of the busy Khlong San Sap which also used to be a centre of traditional silk weaving. Thompson was a knowledgeable collector of Southeast Asian art and antiquities and the house contains some fine stone carvings, Buddha heads and traditional Thai paintings. There is an easy informality to the whole place — it feels almost as though Thompson himself has just popped out for a moment. In reality, this was what he did in 1967, except that he never came back — while on a walk, he disappeared without a trace in Malaysia. Access to the house is not permitted without a guided tour. There is also a gift shop and café, in a Thai-style building, located just inside the gates.

Jim Thompson's House
Opening times: 9am to 5pm daily, guided tour compulsory, last tour 5pm, no photography in the house
Admission: B100, concessions B50

Jim Thompson's House

Note: Jim Thompson
Born in Delaware, USA, in 1906, Jim Thompson had worked as an architect in New York before coming to Thailand in 1945 as the Bangkok head of the Office of Strategic Services, an early version of the CIA. In 1948 he founded the Thai Silk Company Ltd, and almost single-handedly revived an ailing industry. He was still in his prime when he disappeared quite suddenly in Malaysia's Cameron Highlands in 1967. There was speculation that he got lost, and subsequently perished, in the jungle. CIA involvement was even suspected, and the murder of his sister in the USA the previous year only served to fuel the rumours. The most likely theory — if a little mundane — is that Thompson was the unfortunate victim of a hit-and-run accident, and his body then buried to cover up the deed.

Siam Paragon

Siam Square

Retrace your steps down Soi Kasem San 2 until you emerge onto Rama I Rd again, then turn left and follow it until the junction with Phayathai Rd. Siam Square is across this junction to the left. This isn't a square in the usual sense, but actually a grid of small *sois* between Chulalongkorn University and Rama I Rd. Located just opposite the Siam Centre, one of Thailand's first shopping centres, and beside a number of popular cinemas, this open-air square is packed with small shops and stalls selling music, books, accessories and clothing. A number of young Thai designers also sell their work here. This area has become something of a new city centre of sorts, being the Skytrain interchange.

Across Rama I Rd from Siam Square there are a number of upmarket shopping centres, including the older Siam Centre as well as the newer Siam Discovery Centre and Siam Paragon complexes. Siam Paragon is also home to Siam Ocean World, a massive aquarium which is a huge attraction especially during weekends for families with children. Besides the obligatory underwater tunnel, there is a massive eight-metre-deep tank with a coral reef. A smaller tank also offers visitors the opportunity to touch sea creatures such as starfish.

Siam Ocean World
Opening times: 9am to 10pm daily
Admission: B280

Note: Skytrain
Elevated on a pre-stressed concrete viaduct supported by massive columns supporting spans of anything from 35 to 60 metres, the Bangkok Skytrain follows two of the city's main arterial routes, Silom and Sukhumvit Rds, transforming certain parts of them into sunless chasms. Delightfully, the new elevated public spaces which have been created on the 23 station platforms 12 metres above street level reveal Bangkok to be a far greener city than is at first apparent. With an average travelling speed of 35 kilometres per hour (or three times faster than the usual pace of cars in the city), the Skytrain indeed makes for a convenient and pleasant means of commuting.

Prathunam

Chulalongkorn University

Wander the different *sois* of Siam Square at will, and when you're ready to leave, go back out onto Phayathai Rd and turn left. There, Chulalongkorn University takes up most of the left hand side of the road after Soi Chulalongkorn 62. Enter the campus by the gates overlooking the park and lake. Founded in 1916 by Rama VI, and named in honour of his father King Chulalongkorn (Rama V), Thailand's oldest and most prestigious university covers two blocks of the city's downtown. The university's central gardens, between Phya Thai and Henri Dunant Rds, are the site of several attractive buildings, many of which are in the Rattanakosin-style, an attractive hybrid of Thai and Western architecture, and there is a large lake which is often used during the Loy Krathong festival. Home to a number of museums and galleries, the university also contains an auditorium, which is mainly used for classical concerts. It is a pleasant place to stroll in, especially during term time when the neatly uniformed students can be seen milling around the grounds.

Note: Loy Krathong Festival

This national festival originated in the north of Thailand and pays homage to Mae Khong Kha, the goddess of rivers and waterways. In the evenings of the full moon during the 12th lunar month (November), people gather at rivers, lakes and ponds to float *krathongs*, which are small lotus-shaped baskets containing flowers, incense and candles. Places like Chiang Mai and particularly Sukhothai are the best places to experience the sights of this festival.

Wat Pathum Wanaram

Wat Pathum Wanaram

Wander around the Chulalongkorn University campus at will, exiting via Henri Dunant Rd and turn left. Walk all the way to the end of the road and turn right onto Rama I Rd and you will see Wat Pathum Wanaram on your left. This temple, with its delightful cluster of buildings asymmetrically arranged among mature trees and shrubs, and sitting overlooking a small canal, is unlike any of the others in the city. It does not feel urban or hemmed in despite opening onto a busy road and being overlooked by the Skytrain and surrounding skyscrapers. It is home to the Phra Meru Mas, which is a reconstruction of the late Princess Mother's crematorium. Supposed to represent Mount Meru, the mythical home of the gods, it is a rare example of ancient craftsmanship, featuring ornate stencils and lacquered sculptures. Following the Princess Mother's cremation at Sanam Luang in 1996, her remains were transferred here in an elaborate procession. She was particularly revered, for although being born a commoner she was the mother of two kings, Rama VIII and his brother, the current king, Rama IX.

Prathunam

Erawan Shrine

Erawan Shrine ⭐

Leaving the temple complex, turn left onto Rama I Rd and the Erawan Shrine will be across the busy junction of this and Ratchadamri Rds. This garish L-shaped shrine is one of the best known in the city, mainly because of its prominent location on a busy corner outside the Grand Hyatt Erawan Hotel. It dates from the 1950s when a number of accidents occurred while building the hotel, so a shrine to Brahma and Erawan (his elephant mount) was erected to try and appease the bad spirits. The accidents stopped, causing the shrine to rapidly gain a reputation as a place to seek divine intercession. Busy day and night, the faithful come to light incense and pray. Devotees who have had their prayers answered often pay the colourfully dressed temple dancers to perform in thanksgiving. It is interesting to observe that even passing motorcyclists temporarily abandon their handlebars to make the traditional *wai* of respect as they pass at full speed! For a good view of the shrine, climb onto the elevated pedestrian walkway crossing this busy junction.

Note: Makrut

Thai chess, or *makrut*, is played everywhere in Bangkok, and at all times of the day and night. More like a simplified version of the Japanese game of Go than Western chess, it is often played on sheets of tattered cardboard with bottle caps for pieces.

Prathunam Market

With your back to the Erawan Shrine, walk up Ratchadamri Rd, cross the bridge over Khlong San Sap onto Ratchaprarop Rd and you will see the Prathunam Market on your left. This popular market occupies a maze of covered stalls and takes up most of this city block. *Prathunam* means 'water gate' in Thai and refers to the canal lock which used to be located on Khlong San Sap here. Also known as Chalermlok, the market is a favourite shopping place for the locals as it stocks a range of general domestic items. It is a particularly good go-to spot for cheap Indian fabrics and sewing accessories.

Should hunger pangs hit after all that shopping, Prathunam Market is also popular as a late-night eating haunt. Long after the nearby bars and cinemas have closed, its myriad noodle shops and food stalls stay open, serving up supper and snacks.

Baiyoke Tower II

Continue along Ratchaprarop Rd and take the first roadway to your left where the 309-metre-high Baiyoke Tower II looms ahead. The Baiyoke Towers I and II were designed by Bangkok-based Plan Architecture, and the balconies on the first tower have been painted a rainbow range of colours that seem to dissolve into one another as they ascend the building. The Baiyoke Tower I was once the tallest structure in the city, but it was quickly surpassed by the number of newer developments that sprang up in the area. However, its follow-up namesake, the Baiyoke Tower II, has the distinction of being the tallest building in Thailand. Though its pinnacle could have been a little more elegant, the Baiyoke Tower II remains an impressive sight nevertheless.

Baiyoke Tower II

The 400-room Baiyoke Sky Hotel occupies the 22nd to the 50th floors and offers guests a birds-eye view of the cityscape. But for truly hard-to-beat panoramic views, the observation deck at the 84th storey is the place to be, especially on a haze-free day. The glass-panelled access lift that rapidly climbs one of the building's corners is another source for an aerial thrill.

Baiyoke Tower II
Opening times: 10am to 10pm daily
Admission: B200 (includes one drink at the bar on 83rd floor)

Link to the Wireless Road walk: Walk back along Ratchaprarop Rd, turn left onto New Petchburi Rd and then right onto Wireless Rd.

Wireless Road

Nearest Skytrain Station: Chidlom
Approximate walking time: 45 minutes

Downtown East

Wireless Road and its surrounding area is home to a number of embassies as well as some of the city's top hotels. To the rear of the Swissôtel is the little known Nai Lert Shrine, while the road itself, known in Thai as Thanon Witthayu, was originally a narrow tree-lined track between two canals, sadly long since culverted. The area is also home to Lumphini Park, Bangkok's largest park and a delightful green lung in this overcrowded city.

THE WALK

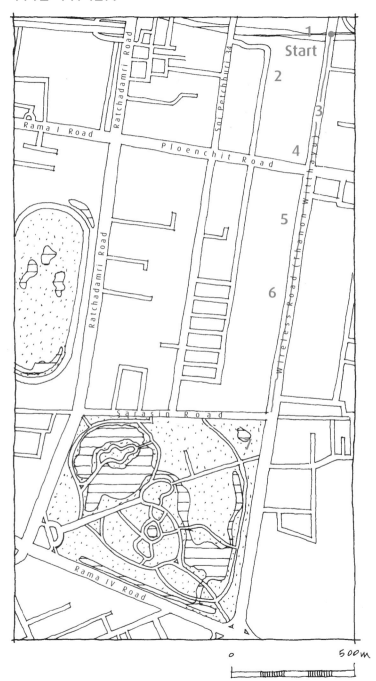

KEY

1. Khlong San Sap
2. Nai Lert Park Shrine
3. Wireless Road
4. British Embassy
5. Royal Netherlands Embassy
6. US Embassy
7. Lumphini Park

Seamstress on street

Khlong San Sap

If you are walking from Chidlom Skytrain station, follow Ploenchit Rd away from the direction of Ratchadamri Rd, then turn left onto Wireless Rd and you will come to the bridge over Khlong San Sap. This canal is an important arterial route and is one of only two major east-west canals that survive in Bangkok. It is a continuation of Khlong Mahanak and runs east through an area of marshland where Rama I banished the Muslim prisoners he captured during one of his southern campaigns — their descendants still live in an enclave on the north bank of the canal, roughly opposite Jim Thompson's House. The Prathunam district takes its name, which means 'water gate', from the canal lock that used to be located here.

Khlong San Sap

Note: Thai Royalty

The Chakri dynasty held absolute power for the first 150 years of its existence, and it still reigns today in the person of Rama IX. The first three kings tried to recreate their fallen capital of Ayutthaya in Bangkok, with Rama III's reign being marked by a strong Chinese influence. Rama IV, particularly after the signing of the Bowring treaty and other similar agreements, ensured that Siam no longer looked inwards and to the past, but outwards, particularly towards the West, and his capital began to reflect this. Rama V's long reign, during a time of political difficulty in Southeast Asia, saw a continued expansion and a marked modernisation of the capital. The 20th century saw an explosion in Bangkok's growth, particularly the second half of the century which has blighted to a shameful extent what used to be a garden city crossed by numerous tree-lined canals.

Nai Lert Park Shrine

Continue along Wireless Rd and you will come to the Swissôtel. This 344-room luxury hotel is housed in a low-rise steeply angled building and set in lush grounds. It is also home to a variety of excellent bars and restaurants. Of greater significance to the locals though, is a sacred shrine that is found here.

At the back of the hotel compound, opening onto a small winding *soi*, is Nai Lert Shrine. Dedicated to Chao Tuptim, a female animist spirit believed to reside in the old banyan tree here, this cluttered little shrine is famous for the hundreds of colourful stylised phalluses, mostly made of wood, which have been donated by grateful parents, invariably mothers. However, the faithful of both sexes pray here at equal measure too, as the Thais believe the phallus is not just a fertility symbol, but also one that also ensures prosperity.

Banyan tree shrine

Shrine, Nai Lert Park

BRACKEN JULY '01

Villa, Wireless Rd

Wireless Road

Return to Wireless Rd and turn right. Still a relatively attractive and architecturally intact street, Thanon Witthayu, as it is called in Thai, is wide and well shaded by mature trees. Running from Petchburi Road in the north to the southeast corner of Lumphini Park, the road is home to a number of embassies, notably the American and British Embassies, both of which

BRACKEN JUNE '09

occupy large compounds. While some of the spacious villas built by wealthy foreigners have been replaced by office towers and luxury hotels, there are still enough remaining to give a flavour of what this fashionable district must have looked like a century ago, a time when the parallel side lanes running along this road used to be *khlongs*.

Cenotaph, British Embassy

MCM
XIV

1939

British Embassy

Follow Wireless Rd to the junction with Ploenchit Rd and the British embassy compound will be on your right, on the corner of Ploenchit and Wireless Rds. With its grandeur, this symmetrically laid-out collection of buildings could be mistaken for the residence of one of the minor members of the Thai royal family. Within sight at the main gates is the focal point of an elegant cenotaph commemorating the British who lost their lives in World Wars I and II. The grounds are open to the public the third Saturday of November each year for a hugely popular charity fair.

Royal Netherlands Embassy

Crossing Ploenchit Rd, continue down Wireless Rd and you will see the gates leading to the winding driveway of the Netherlands Embassy about halfway down the road on your right. The attractive wooden building has a tower and sits in beautifully landscaped grounds. It takes pride of place as one of the few such lavish embassies to remain in the city, having escaped a fate as a commercial development site. The nearby Spanish Chancellery was demolished for this purpose in the 1990s. Most countries' embassies that were privileged to own land have similarly sold their large plots for a generous profit and leased offices in more convenient office buildings.

> **Did You Know?**
> Thailand's royal family has a strong American connection: Rama IX, the present king, was born in America, as was his brother, Rama VIII. The King's eldest daughter was previously married to an American.

US Embassy

Continue along Wireless Rd, where the US Embassy will be on your right, just after the US Ambassador's residential compound. While the street is pleasant, the embassy of the world's superpower pales in comparison as it has the uniform barracks appearance of its native counterparts around the world. Offering some redemption is the US Ambassador's Residence which is in stark contrast to the embassy and more in harmony with the city. Pretty, small in scale, and with a number of unostentatious but comfortable-looking wooden villas dotted around a large, tree-shaded compound, it is easily visible from the road and is a throwback to what the district looked like originally.

Lake, Lumphini Park

Lumphini Park

Keep strolling along Wireless Rd and you will see Lumphini Park on your right. Named after the Buddha's birthplace in Nepal, Lumphini Park was conceived by Rama VI and intended as the site of a national exhibition, but plans fell through after his death. A statue of the king at the Silom Rd corner of the park continues to honour the memory of its nature-loving creator.

Even though Lumphini Park has lost some of its perimeter to carparks and even a number of ugly buildings, it remains the largest single public green space in the city. It has two boating lakes, islands (some with quaint bridges), as well as several pagodas and pavilions, one of which was built to commemorate King Rama IX's 72nd birthday. The early morning is the busiest but best time to visit the park, with joggers, hoards of pyjama-clad Chinese practising *tai chi chuan*, and other visitors enjoying use of the park's popular outdoor gym.

Lumphini Park
Opening times: 5am to 7pm daily
Admission: free

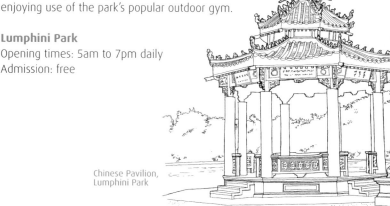
Chinese Pavilion,
Lumphini Park

Link to the Silom Road walk: Exit Lumphini Park at the Rama IV and Wireless Rds junction and turn right onto Sathorn Rd.

Silom Road

Downtown South

The commercial heart of Bangkok, the Silom Road area is home to myriad offices, shops and restaurants. Towards the river end of the road, and also on parallel Suriwong Rd, a number of shops specialise in gems, antiques and silk. The night market on Patpong Sois 1 and 2 draws huge crowds every night (except Wednesdays, when it is closed), while the stretch of road between Patpong and Lumphini Park is home to some of the city's most popular bars and nightclubs, some of the more colourful variety. Silom Rd also has contrasting surprises such as a large Christian cemetery which has borne witness to the vicinity's marked transformation.

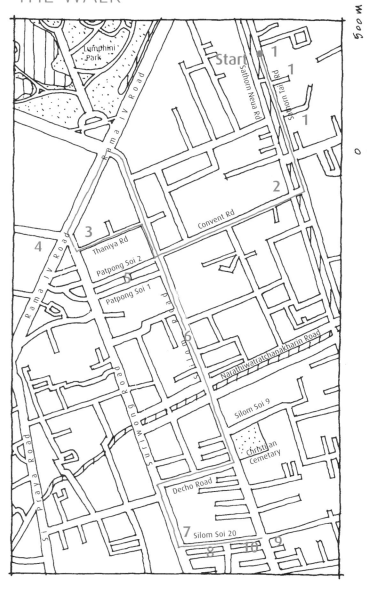

Start

Lumphini Park

Rama IV Road

Sathorn Neua Rd

Sathorn Tai Rd

Convent Rd

Thaniya Rd

Patpong Soi 2

Patpong Soi 1

Silom Road

Surawong Road

Narathiwatratchanakharin Road

Silom Soi 9

Christian Cemetery

Decho Road

Silom Soi 20

Si Phraya Road

500m

KEY

1. Sathorn Road
2. Christ Church
3. Jim Thompson's Thai Silk Company
4. Queen Saovapha Snake Farm
5. Patpong Night Market
6. Silom Road
7. Neilson-Hays Library
8. Mirasuddeen Mosque
9. Sri Mahamariamman Temple
10. Silom Village

Sukhothai Hotel

Sathorn Road

If you are walking from Sala Daeng Skytrain station, follow Convent Rd to the end and turn left onto Sathorn Rd. This was once an elegant, tree-lined boulevard but in recent decades it has descended into a traffic-choked mess. At the beginning of the 20th century this was the fashionable heart of expatriate life in Bangkok, with large villas sprawled across spacious tree-shaded grounds. Most of these have now been replaced by hotels and office towers, but a few, like the Russian Embassy, remain and give a hint of what life must have been like for the privileged foreign residents of Bangkok over a century ago.

The southern side of Sathorn Rd is where some of the city's most exclusive and beautiful hotels can be found. The **Sukhothai** is a stylish 224-room hotel with an understated elegance that is both modern and yet distinctly Thai. Its long, low buildings have shady colonnades overlooking beautiful pools and gardens, some of which feature traditional-looking *chedis*. The hotel's interior makes generous use of shimmering silk on its wall panels and has an impressive collection of contemporary terracotta bas-reliefs replicating those found in Sukhothai, Thailand's ancient capital. The hotel's Sunday brunch has become a Bangkok institution.

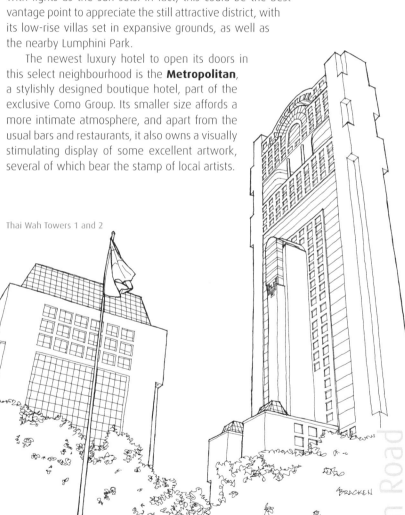

Slightly farther along Sathorn Rd are the two Thai Wah Towers, with the 32nd to the 60th floors of the taller skyscraper housing the **Westin Banyan Tree Hotel**. Guests almost certainly seize the opportunity to experience the hotel's spectacular open-air swimming pool in the multi-storey opening punched high up through the fabric of the building. Indeed, the pool area is a pleasant place to linger over a cocktail and watch the nighttime cityscape come alive with lights as the sun sets. In fact, this could be the best vantage point to appreciate the still attractive district, with its low-rise villas set in expansive grounds, as well as the nearby Lumphini Park.

The newest luxury hotel to open its doors in this select neighbourhood is the **Metropolitan**, a stylishly designed boutique hotel, part of the exclusive Como Group. Its smaller size affords a more intimate atmosphere, and apart from the usual bars and restaurants, it also owns a visually stimulating display of some excellent artwork, several of which bear the stamp of local artists.

Thai Wah Towers 1 and 2

BRACKEN

Silom Road

Christ Church

Continue along Sathorn Rd and turn right at the junction with Convent Rd. You will see the delicate gothic-style Christ Church upon the corner. This quaint and pretty church looks rather like an Anglican parish church, and seems, as a result, a little misplaced among the swaying palm trees. It was built in 1904 with Rama V's permission as an ecumenical site of worship for the large Christian community then living in the area. Convent Rd took its name from the Carmelite convent and school that are still located halfway down this tree-lined street.

Christ Church

Jim Thompson's Thai Silk Company

Follow Convent Rd to the end and turn right onto Silom Rd, then take the next left onto Thaniya Rd. Follow it to the end and turn right onto Suriwong Rd; Jim Thompson's Thai Silk Company will be on your right. The flagship store of this exclusive chain, this handsome building is built in the style of 17th-century Ayutthaya and is a Suriwong Rd landmark. It opened in 1967, just two weeks before the American magnate himself mysteriously disappeared in Malaysia. The showrooms continue his enduring legacy and offer a tempting array of Thai silk in its many forms — from clothing and accessories, to bolts of raw fabric for use in tailoring or home furnishing. Café 9, a coffee shop decorated in the style of Jim Thompson's House, is located on the second floor.

Jim Thompson's Thai Silk Company

Queen Saovapha Snake Farm

Turn right after you leave Jim Thompson's Thai Silk Company and you will see, across Rama IV Rd in front of you and on the left-hand side of Henri Dunant Rd, the Queen Saovapha Snake Farm. Originally called the Pasteur Institute, it was renamed in honour of the wife of Rama V. Run by the Thai Red Cross, it is home to a better collection of snakes than even Dusit Zoo, while its

Silom Road

Chulalongkorn Hospital

emphasis, unlike other Thai snake farms, is on education, with a slideshow before its demonstrations of venom milking (twice daily on weekdays and once a day on weekends). The snake venom is used in the production of anti-snake-bite antidotes.

Across Henri Dunant Rd from the snake farm is **Chulalongkorn Hospital**, a series of fine European-style neoclassical buildings, with some of their elements, like the overhanging eaves, adapted to suit the tropical climate. These are generally in quite good condition, but as the busy hospital has had to upgrade itself over the years, some of the earlier buildings have received insensitive add-ons. As a result, these architectural gems, especially the one whose side faces onto Lumphini Park, can hardly be seen anymore.

Queen Saovapha Snake Farm
Opening times: 8:30am to 4:30pm, Mon to Fri; 8:30 to noon, Sat, Sun and public holidays (shows 10.30am and 2pm, Mon to Fri; 10.30am, Sat, Sun and public holidays)
Admission: B70

Patpong Night Market

Continue along Rama IV Rd in the direction of Lumphini Park, then take the next right, a sharp turn, onto Silom Rd. Follow the road until you come to Patpong Soi 2, which will be on your right just after Sala Daeng Skytrain Station. These *sois* take their name from their original owner and developer, a Chinese businessman called Patpongpanit. They remain privately owned and

have become one of the city's most popular night markets (as well as one of the world's most notorious red-light districts). Patpong is best known for its counterfeit goods — everything from clothes to watches and music — and is slowly encroaching on the neighbouring stretches of Silom Rd. This area first became popular in the 1960s, when American soldiers on leave from active service in the Vietnam War travelled here for rest and recreation. In the 1990s, more fashionable bars and nightclubs began to carve a niche for themselves among the sleazy go-go bars and massage parlours, even though these are still thriving. Silom Sois 2 and 4 have a lively gay scene, which is quite open and generally very mixed, while Thaniya Rd is almost exclusively Japanese, to the extent that other nationalities are even barred from entering some of the entertainment establishments.

Patpong Night Market
Opening times: 9pm to 2am daily, except Wed
Admission: free

Silom Road

Wander the lanes and alleyways of Patpong and when you're ready to leave, head back out onto Silom Rd and turn right. This is a narrow street lined by increasingly tall buildings. The northern part of the road is further darkened by the Sala Daeng Skytrain Station. Home to fashionable offices, shops and restaurants, it's hard to believe that just a generation or two ago this was a canal with orchards on either side. A faint reminder of those days is the sight of thousands of barn swallows that come to nest in the few remaining trees between October and March.

Walk along Silom Rd, away from the Sala Daeng Skytrain Station, and you will come to the whimsical little windmill sculpture sitting at the heart of the busy junction of roadway and water where Silom Rd crosses the canal at Narathiwatratchanakharin Rd. This sculpture obviously takes its name from Silom Rd — *Silom* being Thai for windmill. Located on either side of Silom Soi 9 (Soi Suksa Witthaya), which is the next left after Narathiwatratchanakharin Rd, are Christian cemeteries. Rundown but charming, these used to be the property of Assumption Cathedral, which is located not too far away, just off Soi Oriental (Charoen Krung Soi 40). Burials were active since the 1950s, but new zoning laws in the 1990s forbade this in central Bangkok, which also means that all existing remains will have to be exhumed and interred elsewhere eventually. Some of the cemeteries' monuments are quite impressive, particularly the Xavier Crypt, which consists of a large white octagon sitting at the heart of the second graveyard and directly in line with the pitched-roofed wooden gateway.

Farther along Silom Rd, just past the Christian cemeteries, there is a small Chinese cemetery with an elegantly decorative gateway.

Windmill

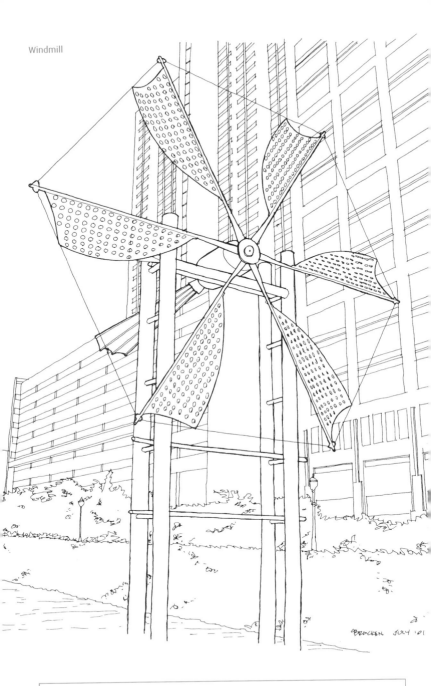

Did You Know?
Silom means 'windmill' in Thai, and this roadway derives its name from the water pumps that used to be located in the area.

Neilson-Hays Library

Turn right off Silom Rd onto Decho Rd and follow it to the end. Make a left onto Suriwong Rd and the Neilson-Hays Library will be on your left, at the corner of Suriwong Rd and Soi Pradit (also known as Silom Soi 20). Housed in an elegant building next door to the British Club, this library's 20,000 volumes form one of Southeast Asia's finest English-language collections. It was built in 1921 to honour the memory of Jennie Neilson-Hays, who was the mainstay of the Bangkok Library Association from 1895 to 1920. The library's rotunda is also home to a modern-art gallery.

Neilson-Hays Library
Opening times: 9:30am to 5pm, Tue to Sun (closed on public holidays)
Admission: free

Neilson-Hays Library

Mirasuddeen Mosque

Turn left onto Soi Pradit (Silom Soi 20) and halfway along you will see the Mirasuddeen Mosque on your right. Thailand has a significant minority population of Muslims, mostly from the south, and particularly in Pattani. Until the beginning of the 20th century this province was an independent sultanate owing tribute to Siam, and there remain a good number of Muslim enclaves dotted around the city. This mosque was built in the 1990s by an Indian who dedicated himself to Bangkok's Muslim community. The building faces a Muslim charity organisation which helps the poor, educates children, and even collects bodies of the deceased which go unclaimed in the city.

Mirasuddeen Mosque
Opening times: 5am to 8pm daily
Admission: free

Mirasuddeen Mosque

Sri Mahamariamman Temple

Sri Mahamariamman Temple

At the end of Soi Pradit (Silom Soi 20), turn right onto Silom Rd and you will see on your left the Sri Mahamariamman Temple, which is also known as the Maha Uma Devi Temple. After 1858, when India became a British crown colony, a number of Indians decided to move to Bangkok rather than stay in their own country under British rule. Many of them were Tamils, and a group of them founded this colourful Hindu temple in the following decade. The main building of the complex has a gold-plated copper dome behind the six-metre *gopuram* (monumental entrance) featuring various Hindu gods. The Thai name for this temple is Wat Khaek (Guests' Temple), but an underlying cross-cultural heritage embraces both Thai and Chinese devotees who come to worship here. The Hindu deities Shiva and Ganesh are revered by Thai Buddhists, while Hindus regard the Buddha as one of the incarnations of Vishnu. Although always busy, the temple is particularly worth visiting around November when it is lit up for Deepavali (the Festival of Lights). During the rest of the year, an oil lamp ritual is held most middays, and on Fridays at 11:30am there is a *prasada* (vegetarian ceremony), in which food that has been blessed is distributed to devotees.

Sri Mahamariamman Temple
Opening times: 7am to 6pm daily, (Deepavali festival falls around November)
Admission: free

Note: Deepavali
Indian temples and homes are decorated with lights to mark the Indian New Year which is calculated annually according to Indian almanacs, sometimes occurring in October, but more often in November. Also known as the Festival of Lights, this is when Hindus mark Lord Krishna's victory over Narakasura, which is seen as a triumph of good over evil, symbolised by light overcoming darkness.

Silom Village

Almost opposite the Sri Mahamariamman Temple on Silom Rd is the Silom Village Trade Centre, a centre for traditional Thai handicrafts with a number of shops housed in and around one of the few villas here. These have survived from the time when this roadway was a gracious residential district and popular with Westerners. There are also a number of traditional Thai restaurants as well as a small hotel attached to this unusual and pleasant little shopping arcade.

Link to the Charoen Krung Road walk: Follow Silom Rd to the end, turn left onto Charoen Krung Rd and the Bangrak Market will be on your right, between Charoen Krung Sois 44 and 46.

Charoen Krung Road

Nearest Skytrain Station: Saphan Taksin
Approximate walking time: 1 hour

Old European Quarter

This was originally the location of Bangkok's port and became home to an increasing amount of foreign commercial activity throughout the 19th century, which in turn resulted in a number of elegant, colonial-style buildings, starting with the Portuguese Chancellery, built on land granted in 1820, and the French Embassy, built shortly afterwards. Other buildings soon followed in answer to Westerners' increasing needs: these included offices, homes and even the very French-looking Assumption Cathedral which sits on Bangkok's only European-style square.

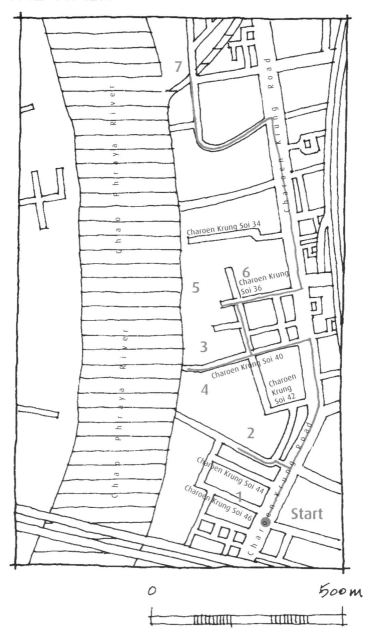

KEY

1. Bangrak Market
2. Wat Suan Phu
3. Oriental Hotel
4. Assumption Cathedral
5. Old Customs House
6. Haroon Mosque
7. Khlong Padung Krung Kasem

Charoen Krung Road

Bangrak Market

If you are coming from the Saphan Taksin Skytrain station, turn left onto Charoen Krung Rd and the Bangrak Market will be on your left, between Charoen Krung Sois 44 and 46. This small but busy market is open every day, and it supplies many of the nearby hotels with fruit, vegetables, meat and seafood. It also has a fabric and clothes section.

Wat Suan Phu

Wander the *sois* between Charoen Krung Rd and the river at will. In the reign of Rama V, sections of the old city wall were demolished to provide foundations for roads, this being the first of them. Loathe to see all traces of the city walls vanish, Rama V preserved two of the original 14 fortified towers: Mahakath Fort near the Golden Mount, and Phra Sumen Fort on Phra Athit Rd are still standing today. Running through the heart of Bangkok's Old European community, from Yannawa in the south all the way through Chinatown to Wat Pho in the north, Charoen Krung (or New Rd as it is also called), was Thailand's first paved highway and it linked the Customs House to the many trading companies in the area. It is still home to many gem and antique traders today. A tramline, started in 1892, also used to run along the road (the last tramline vanished from the city in 1965).

Shophouse, Cheroen Krung Road

While the road itself is choked with traffic, pollution and noise, its side streets — particularly the ones leading to the river — are lined with trees and some really lovely wooden houses and can seem as bucolic as country lanes. It is also a good place to buy gems and antiques, with relatively small shops such as the **House of Gems**, which stocks different types of rocks and fossils, including tektites, which are glassy meteorites that come from Northeast Thailand. On sale are even dinosaur droppings!

Between Charoen Krung Rd and the river runs the narrow Charoen Krung Soi 42. Wat Suan Phu is on the right-hand side of this laneway. A wooden temple with some finely carved details, it is well-known for its Phra Bodhisattvakuan-In, a Chinese shrine positioned over a carp pool.

Oriental Hotel

When you have finished wandering the *sois* between Charoen Krung Rd and the river, return to Charoen Krung Rd and turn left. Follow the road until you come to Soi Oriental (Charoen Krung Soi 40), which will be on your left. Near the end of this *soi* is the Oriental Hotel on your right. One of the world's most celebrated hotels, it was established in 1876 by two Danish sea captains, but owes much of its charm to the Sarkies brothers, originally from Armenia, who completely rebuilt it in 1887 to ensure that it was up to the standard of its sister hotels, the E&O in Penang, and the Raffles in Singapore. Two wings were added in the 20th century: the Tower Wing in 1958, and the River Wing in 1976. Neither of them adds greatly to the hotel's charm, though they fulfill the basic purpose of providing comfortable and pleasant lodgings. Repeatedly voted the world's best hotel, the original white, shuttered building still stands overlooking a small but lavishly planted lawn. This is the wing which contains the Authors' Suites, and is where W. Somerset Maugham stayed while recovering from a bout of malaria back in the 1920s. There is also the Authors' Lounge, where afternoon tea is served and small concerts occasionally performed. Overlooking the entrance to the hotel is China House, one of Bangkok's most lavish restaurants. Located in a pretty little house dating from the reign of Rama VI, the interior was designed to evoke 1930s' Shanghai. The neighbouring building, the **Commercial Company of Siam**, was erected at about the same time. Similarly, both structures are built of masonry and have beautifully detailed decorative woodwork.

Note: Writers

Joseph Conrad, in his novel *The Shadow Line*, wrote about journeying up the Chao Phraya River; W. Somerset Maugham described his impressions of 1920s' Thailand in *The Gentleman in the Parlour*, while more recently, Alex Garland gave a brief but devastating description of life on Khao San Rd for backpackers in search of the perfect getaway in *The Beach*. No list of Westerners writing about Bangkok would be complete, however, without Anna Leonowens, the

English governess at Rama IV's court whose memoirs were the basis for the hit musical *The King and I* (which is actually banned in Thailand for what the locals perceive to be an inaccurate portrayal of their much revered king). Conrad and Maugham have had suites at the Oriental Hotel named after them, while other authors so honoured include Noel Coward, Gore Vidal, Graham Greene, James Michener and Barbara Cartland — a mixed bag of writers who may not have contributed anything of particular significance to Thailand's canon other than having the distinction of being former hotel guests. The Oriental would do well to likewise honour some of the country's very own literary greats, of whom two come to mind: S.P. Somtow, whose *Jasmine Nights* remains a delightful read, as well as Kukrit Pramoj, who penned the magnificent *Four Reigns*.

Assumption Cathedral

Across the *soi* from the Oriental Hotel is a wide passageway under a delightful Venetian-style arch which leads to a small pedestrian square presided over by the Assumption Cathedral. This very French-looking brick and stucco building dates from 1910 when it was built on the site of an earlier cathedral. The twin towers of its Romanesque-style façade contrast interestingly with its richly decorated Rococo interior, and which contains a high barrel-vaulted ceiling, decorated appropriately enough in blue and gold, the colours most associated with the Virgin of the Assumption. It is all delicately lit by a large rose window. The rather striking-looking altar is marble and comes from France.

The little square facing the cathedral is unique in the city — its scale and general atmosphere are quite European, so it's a pity that more isn't done with it (though the no-cars rule should remain). The square also happens to be home to a number of other Western-style buildings, including the modern-looking Assumption College, the neoclassical Catholic Mission and the Renaissance-style Catholic Centre, the back of which stretches all the way to the river.

When you've finished wandering around this delightful little enclave, retrace your steps under

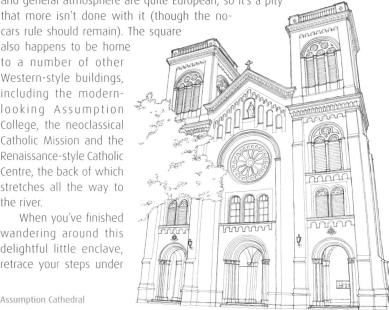

Assumption Cathedral

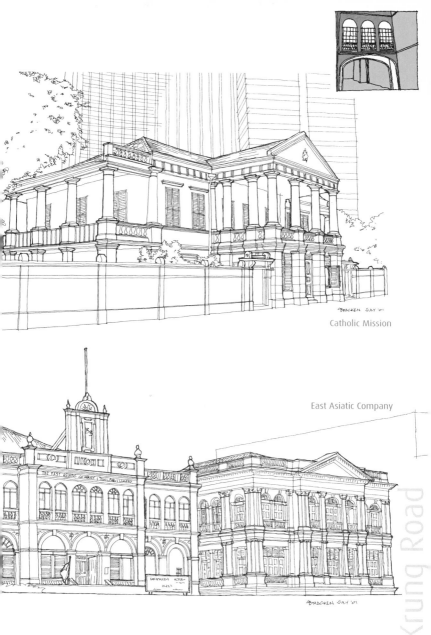

Catholic Mission

East Asiatic Company

the arch, turn left and continue down Soi Oriental (Charoen Krung Soi 40), following it to the end where it overlooks the river. On your left you will see the Venetian-style office building of East Asiatic Company, which was built in 1901. The company itself was founded by Dutch investors in 1897 and still ranks as one of the world's principal trading conglomerates. The plasterwork is very good and the decorative panels over the windows interestingly feature a caduceus. There are plans to turn it into an upmarket shopping centre.

Old Customs House

Retrace your steps back along Soi Oriental and take the first left after the Oriental Hotel, the **French Embassy** will be between the first and second *sois* on your left. For the first century or so of Bangkok's history, all foreign legations were located on or near the Chao Phraya River for the simple reason that the river was the easiest way for representatives to get to and from the Grand Palace on official business. The French have had a long history of diplomatic relations with Thailand, having had an embassy to Auytthaya in the 17th century, while Siam sent an embassy to the court of Louis XIV at Versailles. The French Embassy here is the second oldest in the city (the Portuguese being slightly older). It was built in the middle of the 19th century and has gradually been added to over the years. The building, which has some fine timber fretwork, overlooks a lawn leading down to the water. Along the living quarters on the upper floor runs a broad veranda, which was a common feature of buildings at the time because it was effective for shading, air circulation, and offered protection from flooding.

Turning left after the French Embassy, follow Charoen Krung Soi 36 to the end, where, on your left, overlooking the river, you will see the **Old Customs House**. Though badly neglected, this 19th-century building is one of the finest remaining European structures in the city. Built in the 1880s, it was once the Thai Customs Department, and is now home to a fire brigade. The Treasury Department has recently registered the building with the Fine Arts Department as an historic site, and private investors are said to be interested in its renovation and conversion into a Thai cultural centre.

Haroon Mosque

Backtrack along Charoen Krung Soi 36, past the French Embassy on your right, and cross the small junction of *sois* in front of it where you will see the Haroon Mosque on your left. This tiny mosque is aligned towards the holy city of Mecca and sits at the heart of a small Muslim enclave. Behind it also lies a small Muslim graveyard. Most of the surrounding houses are wooden, and many are quite beautifully detailed, with delicately carved fretwork on fascias and grilles. Most are crammed together with their doors left open, offering glimpses into the inhabitants' way of life, but some of them are quite large and handsome, sitting within their own compounds and surrounded by lush tropical greenery.

Across the *soi* from the mosque is a small but delightful public garden, full of shady walkways and wooden benches where elderly residents gather to relax and chat. Overlooking the other side of the garden you can see Wat Muang Kae, a lovely wooden Buddhist temple. To get to the *wat*, follow Charoen Krung Soi 36 to the end and turn left onto Charoen Krung Rd. Take the next left onto Charoen Krung Soi 34 and follow it to the end, past a large school. Wat Muang Kae will be at the end of the *soi* on your left.

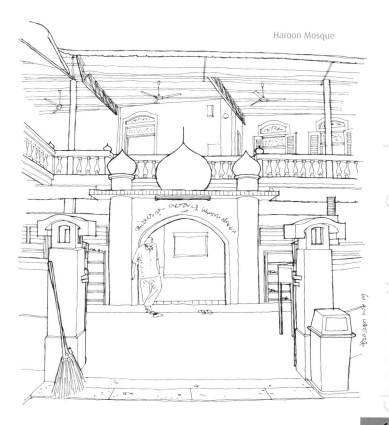

Haroon Mosque

Charoen Krung Road

Khlong Padung Krung Kasem

Retrace your steps along Charoen Krung Soi 34 and turn left onto Charoen Krung Rd, where the rather imposing looking **General Post Office** will be immediately to your left. Set well back from the road, it's a large, rather squat-looking building, decorated with reliefs of *garudas* (mythical beasts: half-bird, half-human), which seem to add to its vaguely fascist air. There is a statue of Rama V in front.

Thailand is well-known for its fine stamps, which are avidly collected all over the world; fittingly, a popular Stamp Market (which also sells coins) is held every Sunday outside the General Post Office. Continue along Charoen Krung Rd and take the second *soi* on the left which is Charoen Krung Soi 30. Just at the point where this *soi* veers sharply to the right you will see the **Portuguese Chancellery**. The Portuguese were the first Europeans to trade with Siam, which they did from their base at

House, Charoen Krung Soi 30

House, Charoen Krung Soi 36

Malacca in Malaysia around the early 16th century. Rama II granted this plot of land to their first consul in 1820, where they erected a "factory", as trading stations were then known, which is now home to the embassy offices. The architectural development of the building is not known for certain, but the original consular residence would most likely have been a simple structure. It was replaced, probably in the mid-19th century when better building materials became available, by the present attractive villa, which faces the river, as most buildings did in those days, with the upper rooms opening onto a wide veranda over the thick-walled lower floor.

Continue along Charoen Krung Soi 30, passing the Royal Orchid Sheraton on your left. Located opposite is a charming symmetrical two-storey neo-classical commercial building, now no longer in use and in need of some repair. Continue along the *soi* and you will come to Khlong Padung Krung Kasem. This quiet canal is one of the longest in the city, being the outermost of three concentric rings dug by Rama I for the defence of his city. Like its sister canal Khlong Bang Lamphoo, this is not so very well preserved, with Khlong Lord retaining the best condition of all three *khlongs* today. Starting at the Thewet Ferry Pier in the north of the city, Khlong Padung Krung Kasem runs southeast past the Thewet Flower Market, crosses Khlong Mahanak and heads south, past the railway sidings at the back of Hua Lamphong Station where it becomes a pretty tree-lined waterway, before disappearing into a culvert near the Royal Orchid Sheraton Hotel from which it debouches into the Chao Phraya River again.

Link to the Chinatown walk: Keeping Khlong Padung Krung Kasem to your left, follow Maha Phrutharam Rd until you come to Hua Lamphong Railway Station.

Khlong Padung Krung Kasem

Chinatown

Sampeng

One of Bangkok's most colourful and vibrant districts, Chinatown, or Sampeng as it is sometimes still known, is full of narrow *sois* teeming with activity, markets with colourful awnings to protect from the sun and rain, food stalls selling an amazing variety of snacks — not all palatable to Western tastes — and, of course, shophouses where traditional Chinese crafts continue to be practised.

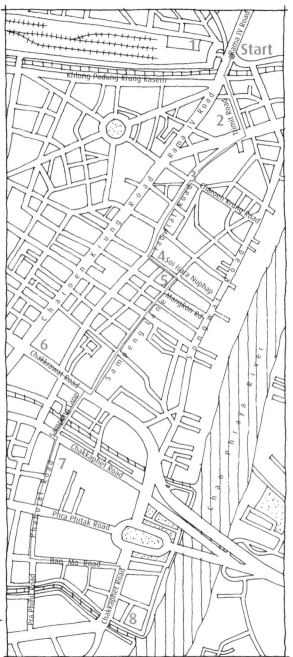

KEY

1. Hua Lamphong Railway Station
2. Wat Trimit
3. Yaowarat Road
4. Kao Market
5. Tang To Kang Gold Shop
6. Nakorn Kasem Market
7. Phahurat Market
8. Flower Market

chinatown

Hua Lamphong Railway Station

If you are walking from the Si Phraya Chao Phraya Express Pier, keep Khlong Padung Krung Kasem to your left and follow Maha Phrutharam Rd until you come to the Hua Lamphong Railway Station. When this historic train station, said to be based on one of the mainline terminals in Manchester, England, was built as Bangkok's main rail junction, it was outside the city centre to the east. It is now to the west of the area known as Downtown, which shows just how much Bangkok has grown and the city centre shifted in the last hundred years. Rama V was a tireless champion of modernisation and built the first railway line in Thailand in 1891, a private one from Paknam to here. Today, trains leave Hua Lamphong travelling to the North, Northeast, the Central Plains and the South. The city's other train station, Bangkok Noi, serves only the South.

Wat Trimit

With your back to Hua Lamphong Railway Station, walk down Trimit Rd and Wat Trimit will be on your right. Also known as the Temple of the Golden Buddha, this Buddhist place of worship is best-known for housing the world's largest solid gold statue of the Buddha. Although the interior is also splendid, the highlight of any visit has to be the temple's famous 18-carat resident gold statue. Four metres in height and weighing five tonnes, it was discovered by accident in 1955 by East Asiatic Company workers who were

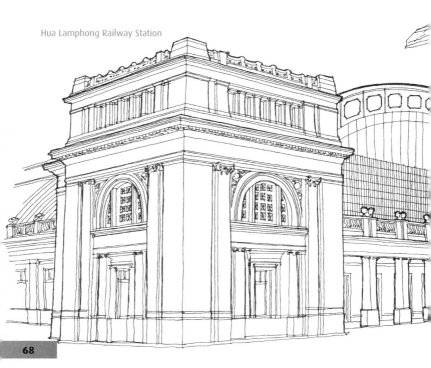

Hua Lamphong Railway Station

Wat Trimit

extending the port of Bangkok. What was unearthed initially seemed to be a plain stucco Buddha dating back to the 13th-century and said to have come from Sukhothai. For the next 20 years or so, the statue was kept at Wat Trimit under a makeshift shelter. When the time came for it to be moved to a more permanent location, its golden identity was finally revealed when its plaster cracked after it slipped from the transporting crane. The statue was probably encased in stucco to deceive thieving Burmese raiders, a common practice during the Ayutthaya period. The Emerald Buddha had also been hidden in such a manner, although during a much earlier period (it too, was discovered to be of great value when its plaster was accidentally flaked off). Today, local Chinese residents come to Wat Trimit to worship and earn merit by rubbing gold leaf onto some of the temple's smaller Buddha images.

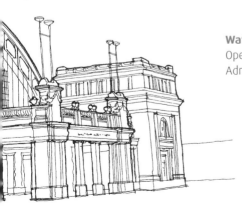

Wat Trimit
Opening times: 9am to 5pm daily
Admission: B20

Chinatown

Yaowarat Rd

Did You Know?

Bangkok's Chinese residents originally lived in Rattanakosin, in the area where the Grand Palace is now located, but when Rama I decided to move his capital from across the river in Thonburi in 1782, the entire community was forced to relocate here.

Yaowarat Road

Walk to the end of Trimit Rd and you will see a tall traditional-looking **Chinese Gate** located at the heart of a small circus where Trimit Rd crosses Charoen Krung Rd, which is also where a number of other smaller streets converge. This attractive and colourful gateway acts as a focal point for the district and is seen as an entry way into Chinatown, an area of the city which has its own unique identity and character. Yaowarat Rd sees Chinatown at its most atmospheric, with garish colours, pungent smells and overwhelming noise everywhere. This roadway is the main route through the district and is lined with goldsmiths, herb sellers, noodle stalls and a wide variety of restaurants, all under huge neon signs where the numerous Chinese characters crowd out the few Thai and English words that can be seen. It looks more like a street in Shanghai or Beijing than Bangkok.

Note: The Chinese

Chinese merchants came to Thailand from the 14th century onwards. During the late-18th and early-19th centuries, following years of war in the country, Chinese immigration was actively encouraged in order to help rebuild the economy. The Chinese went on to integrate into Thai society so successfully that by the middle of the 19th century, half of Bangkok's population could claim to have at least some Chinese blood. Today, the Chinese is still a flourishing ethnic group that continues to dominate Thailand's financial and commercial sectors.

Chinatown Gate

BRACKEN MAY '01

Chinatown

Kao Market

There are some interesting shops on Soi Isara Nuphap, a busy but narrow *soi t*o the left of Yaowarat Rd. These include a small sausage shop, said to date from the 19th century, as well as the Kao Market on the left-hand side of the *soi. Kao* means 'old' in Thai, while the nearby Mai Market translates as New Market. Both of these markets sell a large range of Chinese goods. As far back as the 18th century, Kao Market has been supplying the Chinese

BRACKEN AUG '01

Kao Market

community with a vast range of traditional, ceremonial and decorative items that include everything from lanterns to the paper models used in traditional Chinese cremations. Located in what used to be a red-light district, the markets are also a good place to buy fabrics, toys and household goods. Some of the more unusual items on display are the parts of snakes that are used in traditional Chinese medicine!

Tang To Kang Gold Shop

Continue down Soi Isara Nuphap and turn right onto Sampeng Lane (also known as Soi Wanit 1) and you will see the Tang To Kang Gold Shop on your right near the junction with Mangkon Rd. This seven-storey building used to be Chinatown's Gold Exchange until the late-19th century. The shop itself is a good place for anyone interested in buying gold, and it also contains an intriguing-looking antique water filter.

The area between Sampeng Lane and the river is home to a wide variety of interesting buildings, with structures as diverse as charming old shophouses to huge wooden warehouses. The narrow *sois* that criss-cross this part of town remain much as they must have been in the 19th century, and although it is a busy area, particularly with trucks transporting goods to and from the nearby Ratchawong Pier, a wander around these streets and *sois* can be very rewarding as you will get to see a cross-section of Bangkok life that you'll not be likely to find anywhere else in the city.

Shophouse, corner of Songwat
and Ratchawong Roads

Nakorn Kasem Market

Continue along Sampeng Lane until you come to Chakkrawat Rd and turn right. Nakorn Kasem Market will be on your right at the junction with Charoen Krung Rd. Formerly known as the Thieves' Market because of the amount of stolen goods traded here, it has since reformed and is now home to a range of shops selling metalware, ornaments and musical instruments. This whole stretch of Charoen Krung Rd is filled with enticing smells wafting from the innumerable noodle stalls that line the pavement. The nearby Saphan Han Market, a covered market along both sides of Khlong Ong Ang, specialises in electrical goods.

Nakorn Kasem Market
Opening times: 8am to 8pm daily
Admission: free

Phahurat Market

Retrace your steps down Chakkrawat Rd and turn right onto Sampeng Lane again. This roadway turns into Phahurat Rd which meets Chakkaphet Rd, and where Phahurat Market is located on the left. Phahurat Rd is the core of Bangkok's Indian community, and at its heart lies the traditional Indian bazaar of Phahurat Market, which offers all the sights, sounds and smells of a typical Indian city market.

The market stalls spill out onto the pavement of Chakkaphet Rd with their multitude of wares. There are reams of fabric dedicated to a wide range of purposes, from tableware to wedding outfits. The somewhat claustrophobic upstairs section is devoted to traditional Indian accessories such as sandals and jewellery — all invariably ornate — while the streets surrounding the market are crammed with tiny Indian restaurants and food stalls.

Located to the rear of the market is **Siri Guru Singh Sabha**, a traditional Sikh temple and one of the most important spiritual places for Bangkok's large Indian community. This beautifully decorative four-storey building is topped by a gilded dome and is said to be the second largest Sikh temple outside of India. The temple's most sacred shrine is located on the very top floor, in a spacious hallway strewn with rich oriental rugs. Remember to cover your head before entering the temple.

Siri Guru Singh Sabha

Phahurat Market
Opening times: 9am to 6pm daily
Admission: free

Siri Guru Singh Sabha
Opening times: 8am to 5pm daily
Admission: free

Flower Market

Turn left on leaving Phahurat Market and follow Phahurat Rd until it turns into Phra Phitak Rd. Then take the next left onto Ban Mo Rd, which contains a charming terrace of neoclassical shophouses that runs nearly all the way along the right of this street. Sadly, nearly all of them are in bad state of repair, but they illustrate just how high Bangkok's standard of architecture was in the 19th century.

Shophouse,
Ban Mo Road

At the end of Ban Mo Rd turn right and you will see the Flower Market, or Pak Khlong Market, on your left. This 24-hour specialty market overlooking Chakkaphet Rd is famous for having the widest variety of flowers on sale in the kingdom. Apart from providing the city with wholesale flowers round the clock, the market also stocks fresh vegetables. The best time to visit is around 9am when the widest possible choice of blossoms is on display. Deliveries begin to arrive around 1am and by dawn there is a bewildering array of different blooms; even tulips from the Netherlands. It is possible to buy the flowers individually, in bouquets, or in exquisite basket arrangements.

Flower Market
Opening times: 24 hours daily
Admission: free

Link to the Rattanakosin walk: Follow Chakkaphet Rd across Khlong Lord where it turns into Maharat Rd, at the end of which you will see Wat Pho on your right.

Rattanakosin

Nearest Chao Phraya Express Pier: Rachinee
Approximate walking time: 1 hour

Historic Royal City

This is the heart of the old city of Bangkok. Known as Rattanakosin, this was the centre of the new capital founded by Rama I in 1782 and is full of temples, palaces and museums. It is the spiritual and historic heart of the city, and contains some of Thailand's finest Rattanakosin-style architecture (a mixture of Thai and Western elements that takes its name from this part of the city), the best example being the Grand Palace itself, the grounds of which are also home to Wat Phra Kaeo, home to the country's most venerated image, the Emerald Buddha.

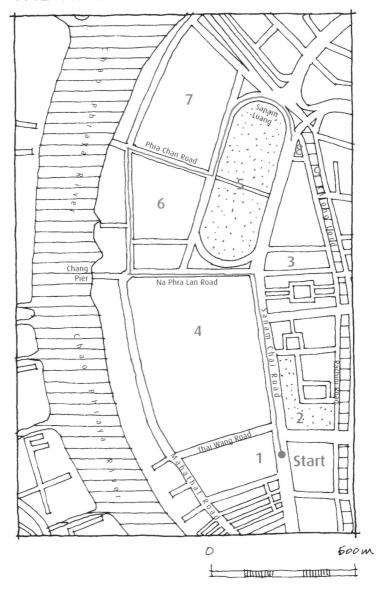

Chao Phraya River

7

Sanam Luang

Phra Chan Road

6

5

8

9

Chang Pier

Na Phra Lan Road

3

Chao Phraya River

4

Sanam Chai Road

Ratchini Road

Thong Lor

2

Thai Wang Road

Mahathat Road

1

Start

0   500 m

KEY

1. Wat Pho
2. Saran Rom Park
3. Lak Muang Shrine
4. Grand Palace
5. Sanam Luang
6. Wat Mahathat
7. National Museum
8. Mae Toranee Fountain
9. Khlong Lord

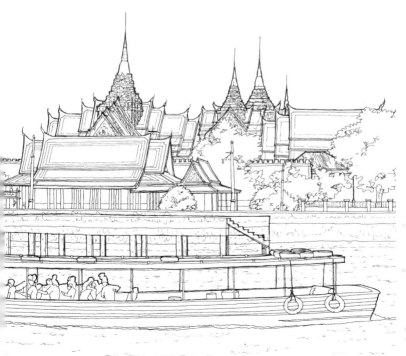

Rattanakosin

Wat Pho

If you are walking from the Rachinee Chao Phraya Express Pier, turn left onto Maharat Rd where Wat Pho will be on your right at the end. Best known as a school for traditional Thai massage, Wat Pho is also a renowned centre for traditional medicine. Officially known to the Thais as Wat Phra Chetuphon, foreigners seem to have clung to their abbreviation of its old name, Wat Photaram. Its other name in English is the Temple of the Reclining Buddha.

This is Bangkok's oldest and largest temple and was originally built back in the 16th century. In the 1780s Rama I rebuilt the original and enlarged the complex. His grandson, Rama III, built the Chapel of the Reclining Buddha in 1832 to house this impressive image, and it was he who turned the temple into a place of learning. Today it is one of Thailand's foremost centres for public education. It has a lively yet lived-in grandeur, but the temple's very popularity detracts from any feeling of reverence the visitor might have been anticipating. All the same, it is a pleasant complex to go on a ramble and contains such fine details as excellent paintings and numerous statues of soldiers guarding doorways, which originally came from China. The monks themselves, some 300 or so of them, live across Chetuphon Rd in the temple monastery.

Wat Pho

Wat Pho
Opening times: 8am to 6pm daily
Admission: B20 (guided tours available, prices vary)

Institute of Massage
Opening times: 8am to 6pm daily (prices vary for massages, learning sessions also available)

Note: Thai Massage
Supposedly dating back 2,500 years, traditional Thai massage is related to Chinese acupuncture and Indian yoga. Wat Pho founded a massage school in the 1960s which has since become the best-known in the city. The temple's highly trained masseurs are skilled in the firm pulling and stretching of the body's limbs that is the hallmark of Thai massage. Visitors can opt for a massage or discover its techniques via the courses conducted at the temple, offered in Thai and English.

Rattanakosin

Saran Rom Park

Diagonally opposite the corner of Wat Pho overlooking the junction of Sanam Chai and Thai Wang Rds is Saran Rom Park. Saran Rom Palace was built in 1866, towards the end of the reign of Rama IV and was originally intended to be the home of the crown prince. However he became king before he could move in, so one of his younger brothers occupied it instead. Rama VI also stayed here while he was crown prince, moving out when he too became king. Around that time the building was given over to its current occupants, the Ministry of Foreign Affairs, and is now used primarily for entertaining important government guests.

The small Saran Rom Park is a quiet place with a Chinese pagoda and other decorative structures. The park is all that remains of the gardens landscaped by Rama IV and which was later turned into a zoo by his son (this was closed when the one at Dusit opened; see page 124). It is all but forgotten now, even though it used to be the site of an important annual fair.

Pagoda, Saran Rom Park

BRACKEN MAY '01

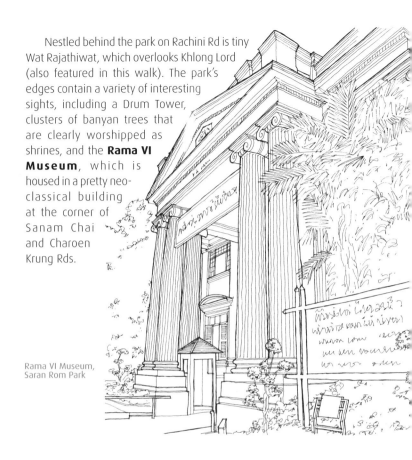

Nestled behind the park on Rachini Rd is tiny Wat Rajathiwat, which overlooks Khlong Lord (also featured in this walk). The park's edges contain a variety of interesting sights, including a Drum Tower, clusters of banyan trees that are clearly worshipped as shrines, and the **Rama VI Museum**, which is housed in a pretty neo-classical building at the corner of Sanam Chai and Charoen Krung Rds.

Rama VI Museum,
Saran Rom Park

Lak Muang Shrine

Exiting Saran Rom Park onto Sanam Chai Rd, turn right and walk until you reach Sanam Luang. The Lak Muang Shrine, which is also known as the City Pillar Shrine, will be on your right. The lovely gardens surrounding this small temple used to be obscured by a petrol station right opposite the Grand Palace. This has fortunately been removed and a new four-metre pillar with a carved lotus-shaped crown has been erected on the site. Known as the Lak Muang, it was placed here to provide a home for the city's guardian spirits — all Thai cities have such shrines. The shrine also incorporates the taller Lak Muang of Thonburi, a district that was recently incorporated into Greater Bangkok. The original City Pillar, containing the city's horoscope, was ceremonially driven into the ground here at 6:45am on 21 April 1782, the astrologically auspicious time and date for the founding of Bangkok. People flock here daily to pray and offer flowers. In one corner of the gardens, classical dancers are paid to perform thanksgiving dances for good fortune attributed to the shrine.

Grand Palace

Facing the southern end of Sanam Luang is Bangkok's most popular tourist attraction, the Grand Palace. It is equally revered in the country itself, with its image even gracing the one baht coin. The royal family no longer lives here, but in the newer Chitrlada Palace in the Dusit district. These days, the Grand Palace is used mainly for ceremonial occasions. Several of the unusual and colourful buildings in the complex are open to the public, including the Phra Maha Monthian Group, the Chakri Group (which contains the magnificent Central Throne Hall) and the Dusit Group.

This vast complex was established in 1782 and is home to a number of royal residences and throne halls as well as government offices and the Temple of the Emerald Buddha. The complex covers an area of approximately 160 hectares (65 acres) and is surrounded by a wall measuring just under two kilometres (about 1.25 miles). Originally the site was home to a 17th-century French fort, at a time when the previous royal palace and its administrative buildings were located across the river in Thonburi. The French were forced to relinquish their stronghold in 1688 when it was discovered that they had been trying to convert the Siamese king to Christianity. The area surrounding the fort had also been home to a large Chinese community, who were forced to relocate to a new site farther down the river, now known as Chinatown. The move was initiated by Rama I's decision to build a new palace complex on the site, and construction began in 1782. The Thai king was instrumental in the choice of site for a number of reasons. First, he considered it an easier location to defend in the event of further attacks by the Burmese.

He also believed it was auspicious for the fresh start he intended to make for the kingdom after the fall of Ayutthya. Finally, the completed complex would also serve as a suitable home for the sacred image of the Emerald Buddha (Phra Kaeo).

The Grand Palace complex was built to be a self-sufficient city within a city, one which the king would never need to leave. He could make public appearances from time to time on a balcony specially constructed for the purpose, which can still be seen overlooking Saran Rom Park, next to the Ministry of Foreign Affairs. The Royal Grand Palace building itself is a hybrid of Thai and Western architectural styles, and is probably one of the best examples of Rattanakosin architecture in the entire country.

Doorway detail, Grand Palace

Rattanakosin

Wat Phra Kaeo (the Temple of the Emerald Buddha) is Thailand's holiest temple, and is home to the country's most sacred image, the Emerald Buddha (Phra Kaeo). Although this complex is referred to as a *wat* (a monastery), no monks actually live here. It was completed in time for Bangkok's centenary in 1882 and formed a focal point for the celebrations. The Emerald Buddha itself is housed in a lavishly decorated *bot*, surrounded by 112 *garudas* (half-man, half-bird) which are shown holding *nagas* (serpents) and are typical of the temple's dazzling decorative details. The upper terrace of Wat Phra Kaeo contains many beautifully gilded figures of Aponsi (half-woman, half-lion). Eight *prangs* border the east of the temple, while the Ramakien Gallery, extending clockwise all around the cloisters, consists of 178 panels depicting the entire story of the Ramakien. The temple's gates are flanked by 12 pairs of demon king statues. The complex also contains a beautiful stone model of Angkor Wat, which was ordered by Rama IV, but only completed during the reign of his successor. From 1769, when King Taksin annexed the provinces of Siam Reap and Battambang, until 1907, when these provinces were ceded to France, Angkor was actually a part of Thailand (when it was known as Siam).

Grand Palace
Opening times: 8:30am to 3:30pm daily (except during certain ceremonies)
Admission: B250 (includes entrance to the Vimarnmek Palace, valid for seven days)

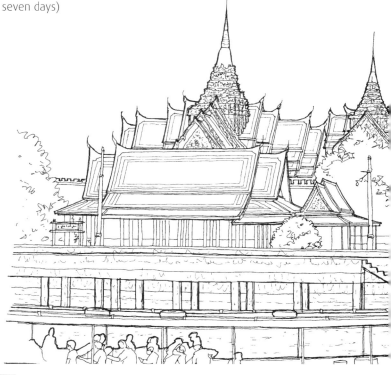

Note: strict dress code: no shorts, short-sleeved shirts or sandals. Visitors can borrow suitable clothing from an office near the Gate of Victory.

Wat Phra Kaeo
Opening times: 8:30am to 3:30pm daily (except during certain ceremonies)
Admission: included as part of the Grand Palace ticket
Note: appropriate dress required and shoes must be removed before entering

Note: The Emerald Buddha
Thailand's holiest image was brought to Wat Phra Kaeo on 5 March 1785 by a grand procession which began across the river at Wat Arun, where it had been kept for the previous 15 years. The first mention of the statue was in 1434 when lightning struck the *chedi* of Wat Phra Kaeo in Chiang Rai, Northern Thailand, revealing a simple stucco image. The abbot of the temple then kept it in his residence until some of the plaster flaked off revealing a jadeite image underneath. The King of Chiang Mai, hearing about the image, sent an army of elephants to retrieve it. Unfortunately for the king, the animal that was carrying the Emerald Buddha refused to go in the direction of Chiang Mai, and the entourage, taking this as a sign, decided to go to Lampang instead. The image moved a number of times during the following century, eventually ending up in Wat Pha Kaew, then Laos in 1552, where it remained until General Chakri (later King Rama I) captured Vientiane in 1778 and took it back to Siam (now Thailand).

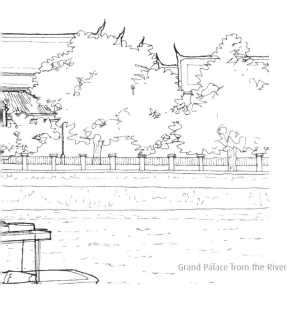

Grand Palace from the River

Sanam Luang

One of Bangkok city centre's few open spaces, this 'field of kings' is the venue for important national ceremonies, such as the royal ploughing ceremony, royal cremations, and the annual kite-flying festival. Rama V was a keen kite-flyer and was glad to allow Sanam Luang to be used for the sport. Fiercely contested kite fights still take place here, usually between February and April. Lined with ancient-looking tamarind trees and surrounded by imposing buildings, including the Grand Palace, the National Museum, National Theatre and National Art Gallery, the Ministry of Justice, two universities and an important temple, Sanam Luang also has a more down-to-earth side, with hawkers on the neighbouring streets selling lotions and amulets, and palm readers and astrologers casting horoscopes. It also used to be the home of the weekend market before it moved to the broader pastures of Chatuchak to the north.

Facing the Grand Palace compound across Na Phra Lan Rd is the **Silpakorn University**, Thailand's most famous fine art school. It was founded in 1943 by Italian artist Corrado Feroci, and the campus includes part of a palace dating from the time of Rama I. A small bookshop just inside the gates stocks books on Thai art in English, while the university often holds art shows in its exhibition hall, with notice boards outside the entrance showing details and opening times. At the end of Na Phra Lan Rd, the area around Chang Pier contains some fine early Rattanakosin-style shophouses, which are now rare in Bangkok and very attractive. A well-established branch of the Bangkok Bank is housed in a similarly handsome corner building.

Sanam Luang

Note: Riverboats

The Chao Phraya River is one of the most important transport arteries in the city for goods and produce as well as for people. Tiny boats laden with all sorts of cargo race across it daily, zipping past the huge rice barges and competing with the numerous ferries for space at the jetties. No visitor can really understand Bangkok until they've seen it from the river, and one of the best and cheapest ways to do this is to catch the Chao Phraya Express. There are also a number of cross-river ferries, as well as plenty of long-tail boats which can be hired privately and make for a good way to see the city's complicated web of *khlongs*.

> **Did You Know?**
> Sanam Luang is regarded as one of the luckiest places in the city because it is home to the Grand Palace, the Lak Muang (City Pillar) Shrine and the Amulet Market.

Wat Mahathat

With your back to the river, turn left onto Maharat Rd where hawkers sell an amazing variety of religious trinkets at the Amulet Market that conducts its business on the pavement on both sides of the road. The market extends all the way from the corner of the Grand Palace compound to Thammasat University. The latter was founded in 1933 and is well-known for its law and political science faculties, it was also the scene of student riots in the 1970s.

The entrance to Wat Mahathat, which is also known as the Temple of the Great Relic, is about halfway down Maharat Rd and to your right. A large complex, it is more notable for its atmosphere, which is beautifully serene, than for its architecture. It was built during the reign of Rama I, and the *wihan* and *bot* were both rebuilt between 1844 and 1851. The *mondop*, which contains the famous relic that gives the temple its name, has a cruciform roof, a feature not often found in Bangkok's temples.

This temple is the national centre for the Mahanakai monastic sect, and its compound contains one of Bangkok's two Buddhist universities. Meditation classes are also held here at 7am, 1pm and 6pm in Section Five, near the monks' quarters. There is also a traditional herbal medicine market, and a weekend market.

Wat Mahathat
Opening times: 9am to 5pm daily
Admission: free

Note: Amulets
Thais can be highly superstitious, and many of them wear amulets as a form of protection. These come in a wide variety of forms and sizes and are sold in specialist markets, often near spiritually significant sites. There are even a number of magazines devoted to them. Although many amulets are religious in nature, tiny images of the Buddha or some other statue are common, while others are more straightforward, such as miniature phalluses, meant to aid fertility.

Mondop, Wat Mahathat

National Museum

With Thammasat University on your left, walk along Phra Chan Rd until you get to Sanam Luang. Turn left and after you pass the university, you will see the National Museum on your left. It is home to one of the largest and most comprehensive collections of art and sculpture in Southeast Asia. Every period of Thai history is represented and it provides an excellent introduction to the arts, crafts and history of the country. Two of the museum buildings, the 18th century Wang Na Palace and the Buddhaisawan Chapel, are particularly worth seeing. The chapel contains the Phra Buddha Sing, which, after the Emerald Buddha, is one of the most venerated Buddha images in Thailand, and is decorated with some of the best Rattanakosin-style murals in the country.

The palace contains an impressive collection of artifacts, with everything from ancient weapons to shadow puppets. Other attractions include galleries of history and prehistory, and the Royal Funeral Chariots Gallery. The frequent guided-tours are free and good, and can help in understanding the collection better, as the labelling in the museum is not always clear. Occupying a large, landscaped corner and overlooking Sanam Luang beside the National Museum is the 500-seat **National Theatre** which specialises in Thai theatrical productions. The building itself incorporates several traditional Thai architectural touches, in this case in the Rattanakosin-style, as do a number of buildings in this part of the city, enlivening what might otherwise be rather bland facades.

Veering right along the top of Sanam Luang you will see the **National Gallery** on your left. This attractive building was built as the Royal Mint in 1902, but became the National Art Gallery in 1977. Its collection consists mainly of modern Thai and international art. Initially, the gallery, like so many others, suffered from lack of funds, but in 1989 new wings were added and now the gracious and well-proportioned rooms frequently feature the work of prominent Asian artists in temporary exhibitions, which are sometimes better than the permanent collection.

National Museum
Opening times: 9am to 4pm Wed to Sun, closed public holidays, English tours 9.30am Wed and Thurs
Admission: B40

National Art Gallery
Opening times: 9am to 4pm Wed to Sun, closed public holidays
Admission: B30

National Art Gallery

Mae Toranee Fountain

Veering right along the top of Sanam Luang you will see the Mae Toranee Fountain on your left across Ratchdamnoen Noi Rd. Originally built by Queen Saovapha, wife of Rama V, to provide fresh drinking water, this statue depicts the earth goddess Mae Toranee and illustrates an ancient Buddhist legend which is popular in temple murals. The story goes that while the Buddha was sitting in meditation, Mara, the force of evil, sent a host of demons to offer him earthly temptations. He remained cross-legged and pointed his right hand towards the ground (the most frequently seen pose of the Buddha in Thailand), calling upon the earth goddess to vouch for his numerous good deeds which had earned him an ocean of water stored in the earth. Mae Toranee obliged by wringing out her hair, and the resultant flow of water engulfed Mara's demons.

Khlong Lord

This is the innermost of the three concentric canals dug for Bangkok's defences by King Rama I. Khlong Lord turned Rattanakosin into an island and even though the waterway is no longer visible north of Sanam Luang, it emerges from its culvert at the Mae Thoranee Fountain and runs due south, passing the Ministries of Justice, Defence and Foreign Affairs as well as Wat Rajapradit, a tiny temple founded in 1864 and built on a foundation consisting of old water jars, before flowing back into the Chao Phraya River at the Rachinee Ferry Pier. To walk along the banks of this canal is to walk through the very oldest part of the city.

Did You Know?
The 'Royal Mile', as the stretch of river that skirts Rattanakosin is known, is actually a canal. It was built in 1534 as a shortcut to eliminate the oxbow which is now known as Khlong Bangkok Noi, and to make it easier for foreign ships to trade with the old capital of Ayutthaya.

Link to Bang Lamphoo walk: Follow Khlong Lord until you come to the bridge at Kalayang Matri Rd, turn left and follow the road as it becomes Bamrung Muang Rd and you will see the Giant Swing directly in front of you.

Bang Lamphoo

Nearest Chao Phraya Express Pier: Chang
Approximate walking time: 1 hour

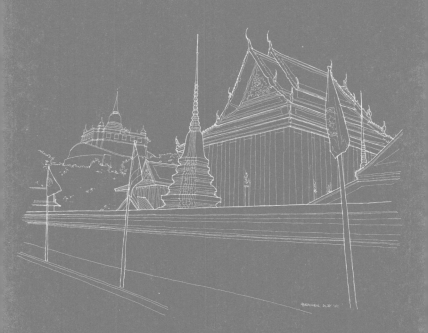

Backpacker District

This area takes its name from the second of three concentric canals dug for Bangkok's defences by King Rama I. Khlong Bang Lamphoo is much less preserved than Khlong Lord, the innermost of the three canals, but it is still a pleasant waterway. The area is also home to some of Thailand's most spectacular temples as well as the Golden Mount, which used to be the highest point in the city. It is now best known for being the haunt of backpackers, with numerous cheap hotels, shops and restaurants all clustered around the near-legendary Khao San Rd.

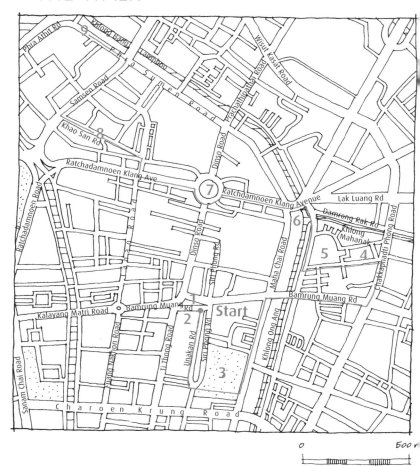

KEY

1. Giant Swing
2. Wat Suthat
3. Romaneerat Park
4. Wat Saket
5. Golden Mount
6. Mahakath Fort
7. Democracy Monument
8. Khao San Road
9. Phra Athit Road

Giant Swing

If you are walking from the Chang Chao Phraya Express Pier, follow Na Phra Lan Rd, then turn right at the corner of the Grand Palace compound, and left onto Kalayang Matri Rd. Follow this road as it turns into Bamrung Muang Rd and the Giant Swing will be directly ahead. *Sao Ching Cha*, as the Giant Swing is known in Thai, was originally built in 1784 by King Rama I and consists of two enormous, slightly-inclined teak posts joined by a carved cross-beam at the top. During ceremonies, which were Brahmin in origin, teams of four would swing in 180-degree arcs while one of the participants tried to bite off a sack of gold hung from the top of 25-metre poles. The event, linked to the veneration of Shiva, caused many deaths and was finally abolished in 1935. The current swing is a replacement of the original and was paid for by the local company founded by the son of Anna Leonowens, the English governess whose memoirs formed the basis of *The King and I*. **Bangkok City Hall**, rather an ugly building, faces onto the square overlooking the Giant Swing.

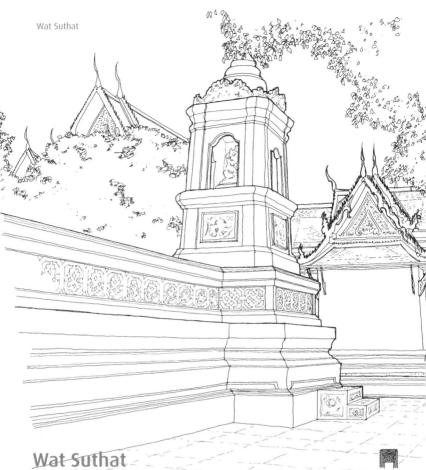

Wat Suthat

This temple, to the right of the Giant Swing and facing the City Hall, is less visited than Wat Pho, even though it is much more impressive. It was founded in 1807 by Rama I and was decorated by his son, but wasn't completed until the reign of his grandson. The artwork and architecture are excellent examples of the Rattanakosin style. The central eight-metre high Buddha is one of the largest surviving Sukhothai bronzes and was moved to Bangkok from Wat Mahathat in Sukhothai by Rama I. The *wihan*, which is the largest in the city, contains murals which are among the most celebrated in Thailand. Amazingly intricate, they depict the Traiphum (Buddhist cosmology) and were restored in the 1980s. The teak doors to the *wihan* are also noteworthy, carved in five delicate layers and standing five-and-a-half-metres tall. One of these, made by Rama II, is now in the National Museum. The cloister around the outside of the *wihan* is lined with 156 golden Buddha images that were supposedly brought to Bangkok as ballast in ships which had carried rice to China. The *wihan* and *bot* are often closed to the public.

Wat Suthat
Opening times: 9am to 9pm daily (except during ceremonies)
Admission: B20

TRACKEN MAY '01

Romaneerat Park

With Wat Suthat on your right, turn right onto Siri Phong Rd and you will see the **Brahmin Temple** on your left. Known as the Dev Mandir Temple and also as the Hindu Samaj, this modern and not particularly interesting-looking building is the centre of Bangkok's Brahmin devotees. The compound is also home to the Bharat Vidyalaya School. Though Brahmanism has been an integral part of Thai royal life since the 14th century (Brahmin priests are still central to certain court functions), few temples in Bangkok exclusively honour the Hindu Trinity of Brahma, Shiva and Vishnu. Brahmanism might seem to be an anachronism in a Buddhist royal court, but is explained by the fact that they originally came to Ayutthaya from Angkor after the Thai conquest of the

Khmer capital and the Ayutthayan kings, in trying to rule the Khmer empire, took over these rites as well, in an effort to legitimise their claim to power. Romaneerat Park, located beside the Brahmin Temple, used to be the site of the Bangkok Remand Prison. In the early 1990s, the prison moved to the Lad Yao District, north of the city, and its grounds converted into this well laid out and beautifully maintained park.

Like its busier counterpart across town, Lumphini Park, this small park also has an open-air gym with excellent views of the nearby Wat Suthat (blaring loudspeakers spoil the bucolic effect — but just a little). The prison watch-towers have been retained, along with some fine old prison buildings, all of which are in excellent condition, sitting amid the canals and the weeping willows. Several elegant late-19th century buildings that are symmetrically arranged around a courtyard act as a rather grand entrance to the park. One of these buildings now houses the Corrections Museum, which contains gruesome but fascinating exhibits, including artifacts and wax models showing past and present execution methods. There are even early-20th-century photographs of a beheading — definitely not for the faint-hearted. The torturing of prisoners to extract confessions was stopped by Rama V due to the cruelty of its methods. One of them involved forcing the accused inside a rattan ball containing spikes, which was then kicked around by elephants!

Romaneerat Park
Opening times: 5am to 9pm daily
Admission: free

Corrections Museum
Opening times: 8:30-4pm, Mon to Fri (closed on public holidays)
Admission: free (no photography allowed)

Did You Know?
Beheading as a means of execution was changed to shooting in 1934. The Thai authorities are currently exploring the possibility of replacing this with lethal injection. Beheadings used to take place in the grounds of the temple which formed part of the prison complex. Shootings now take place close to the temple but no longer on its grounds.

Wat Saket

Exit Romaneerat Park onto Mahachai Rd and turn left. Turn right next onto Bamrung Muang Rd, make a left at Chakkaphatdi Phong Rd and Wat Saket will be on your left. Visitors to this temple usually come to climb the Golden Mount, an artificial hill topped with a golden tower set within its grounds. Most skip a tour of the temple in favour of that novel activity, which is a pity as the building and its compound are rather beautiful.

Originally called Wat Sakae, Wat Saket is one of the oldest temples in Bangkok. Built during the Ayutthaya period, it was significantly rebuilt by Rama I in the late-18th century. It is said that the king, who was then a general, stopped at the temple grounds in 1782 on his way back from Laos with the Emerald Buddha in his possession. He took a ceremonial bath before proceeding to Thonburi, where he was crowned king. The temple's name was subsequently changed to Saket, which means 'the washing of hair'.

During the 19th century, the temple's grounds, being just outside the city walls, served as a crematorium, particularly during epidemics. There were epidemics in Bangkok every 10 years or so until about 1900, and each killed around 10,000 people. During the reign of Rama II, one such outbreak killed more than 30,000 people alone. Their bodies were then removed from the city via the Pratu Pii (Ghost Gate) to be laid on the temple grounds, but the excess number of corpses were unfortunately set upon by dogs and vultures drawn to the stench of death.

Till today, the temple grounds have since been used for more pleasant purposes. A highlight is the annual fair hosted in November with dancing and candlelit processions.

Wat Saket
Opening times: 8am to 6pm daily (annual fair in November)
Admission: free

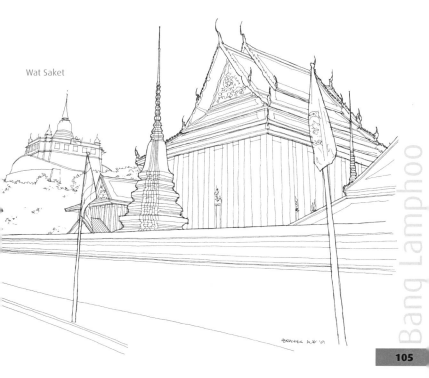

Wat Saket

Golden Mount

Keeping Wat Saket on your right, follow the *soi* until you come to the entrance of the Golden Mount. Rama II was the first king to attempt to build a representation of the mythical Mount Meru here, but the soft soil the city is built on soon led to its collapse. His descendant, Rama V, provided the necessary technology to create the 76-metre mound seen today. The sanctuary at the top of the circular staircase is said to house relics of the Buddha presented to Rama V by the Viceroy of India. The staircase itself is lined with many different and intriguing monuments and tombs, some of which are quite grand. The climb is arduous, but the views from the gallery at the top are worth it, as they take in the whole of the original city centre, including the Grand Palace, Wat Pho and even Wat Arun across the river. It is still the highest point in this part of Bangkok, and until the 1960s it was the highest point in the whole of the city. It has since been overtaken by numerous skyscrapers, but fortunately, doesn't happen to be dwarfed by any nearby.

Pavilion, Golden Mount

Did You Know?
Until the 1960s the Golden Mount was the highest point in Bangkok.

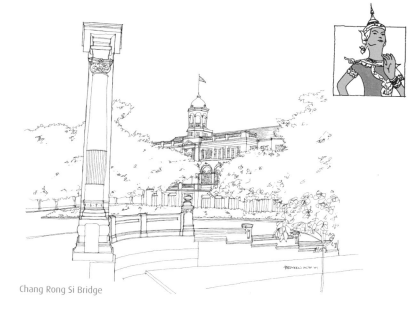

Chang Rong Si Bridge

Mahakath Fort

Exit the Golden Mount compound onto Boriphat Rd, turn right and follow the road across Khlong Mahanak and turn left onto Nakon Sawan Rd. You will see the **Chang Rong Si Bridge** which crosses Khlong Bang Lamphoo here. This is one of the city's most attractive bridges. Its steel structure and concrete slabs are decorated with well-proportioned pillars, curved marble bases and elaborate wrought-iron railings. It was one of the many bridges built by the Department of Public Works, which were designed by Italian engineers and paid for by Rama V himself. The *khlong* here is less well-preserved than the nearby Khlong Lord, the innermost of the three canals, but it is still a pleasant waterway. After passing under Ratchdamnoen Avenue, it splits into two: Khlong Mahanak runs east, while Khlong Ong Ang, a much narrower stretch of water, runs south through Chinatown to the river.

Just beside the Chang Rong Si Bridge lies the restored remains of **Mahakath Fort**, one of only two that have survived, of the 14 originally circling the city. Part of the old city walls also remains standing here and, along with the low tower, look particularly attractive against the backdrop of the Golden Mount. The gates are invariably left open and it is possible to wander along the banks of the Bang Lamphoo, Ong Ang and Mahanak Khlongs.

> **Did You Know?**
> An 1887 survey reported a total of 67 bridges in Bangkok, of which 22 were wooden, and 24 in need of repair. A number of foreign engineers, mostly Italian, were then hired by the Department of Public Works to design new ones. Many of them still stand, with the majority being quite elegant.

Democracy Monument

With your back to the Chang Rong Si Bridge, follow Ratchdamnoen Klang Avenue and you will arrive at the Democracy Monument, which was designed by Silpa Bhirasi, an Italian who subsequently became a Thai citizen and adopted a Thai name. Built in 1939 to commemorate the revolution of 1932, which was when Thailand — or Siam as it was then known — became a constitutional monarchy, it has become the focal point for Thailand's occasional pro-democracy demonstrations. Each of the monument's features is of significance to the revolutionary date, 24th June 1932. The four wing-like towers are 24 metres high, the 75 cannons indicate the Buddhist year 2475 (1932 CE), and the pedestal, which contains a copy of the constitution, is three metres high, referring to the third month of the Thai calendar (June).

When Rama V laid out Ratchdamnoen Avenue he envisaged it to be lined with graceful palaces, but unfortunately the eventual result was considerably less elegant. The repetitive, barrack-like buildings on the inner part of the avenue are the legacy of Field Marshall Phibul, Thailand's dictator during World War II, and tend to be more reminiscent of the grim architecture of Soviet Russia than the elegant structures Rama V must have had in mind. The outer part of the avenue, beyond Khlong Bang Lamphoo, is not much better, home to a number of bland ministerial buildings and a boxing stadium.

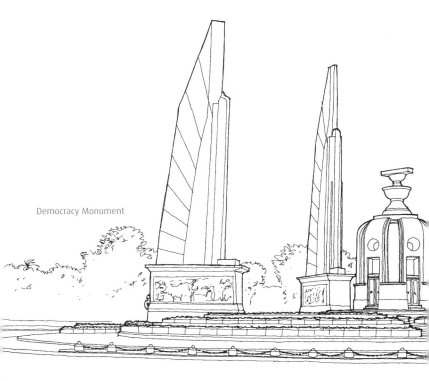

Democracy Monument

Street vendor, Khao San Rd

Khao San Road

Continue along Ratchdamnoen Klang Avenue and on your right-hand side, at the corner of Ratchdamnoen Klang Avenue and Tanao Rd, is **Bo Be Market**, one of the best markets in Bangkok for cloth (it has a particularly fine selection of Chinese silks).

Follow Tanao Rd and turn left onto Khao San Rd, a small street with a somewhat cult status, having been featured in numerous books and films. It has been a favourite haunt of backpackers for decades, with a proliferation of inexpensive guesthouses and eateries. The street is also home to a market which supplies everything a traveller could possibly need, from boots and backpacks to jewellery. It even stocks a good range of music and second-hand books, ideal for long bus journeys up-country or out to the islands.

BRACKEN MAY '01

Phra Athit Road

At the end of Khao San Rd, turn right onto Samsen Rd and left onto Phra Sumen Rd which turns into Phra Athit Rd. At the point where the road veers to the left, you will see the Phra Sumen Fort straight ahead of you. In the late 1990s, this roadway was one of the most fashionable spots to eat and drink in the city, with some even referring to it as Bangkok's Left Bank. Delightful old shophouses and riverside mansions have been renovated to house a vibrant mix of bars, restaurants and shops. It is a popular spot where Thai students, artists and young professionals frequently mingle with the foreigners and expatriates staying at nearby Khao San Rd.

Phra Athit Rd is also home to Suan Santichaiprakarn, a new riverside park established in 1999 to commemorate King Rama IX's then 72nd birthday. The park also includes **Phra Sumen Fort** which is one of just two fortifications in the old city wall that still stands (the other is Mahakath Fort, previously mentioned on page 107). This hexagonal structure was constructed during the reign of Rama I, with its last renovation undertaken in 1999, when the fort was incorporated into the park in honour of the King's birthday.

Link to the Dusit District walk: Retrace your steps along Phra Sumen Rd, then turn left onto Samsen Rd, proceeding to the junction with Wisut Kasat Rd. Turn right and Wat Indrawihan will be on your left.

Dusit District

Nearest Chao Phraya Express Pier: Wisut Kasat
Approximate walking time: 1 hour

New Royal City

The Dusit district is the centre of Thai government and is perhaps the only part of Bangkok to retain some of the city's charm and character prior to the rampant development in the second half of the 20th century. It still remains Bangkok's royal enclave, home to the royal temple of Wat Benjamabopit (the Marble Temple) and the Chitrlada Palace, the royal family's residence. Political power is also concentrated in Dusit, with the National Assembly, Government House, numerous ministries and the Prime Minister's residence all located here. Though the area may seem imposing, it still retains more down-to-earth aspects, with horse-racing at the Royal Turf Club, and Muay Thai boxing at Ratchdamnoen Stadium. It even has a zoo.

THE WALK

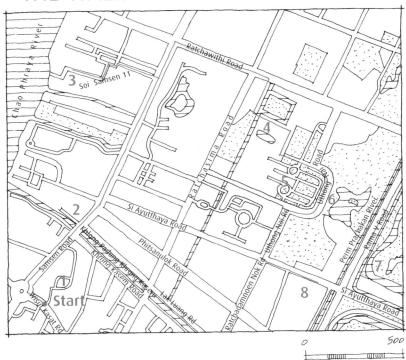

KEY

1. Wat Indrawihan
2. Thewet Flower Market
3. St Francis Xavier Church
4. Vimarnmek Palace
5. Ananta Samakorn Throne Hall
6. Dusit Zoo
7. Chitrlada Palace
8. Wat Benjamabophit

Wat Indrawihan

If you are walking from the Wisut Kasat Chao Phraya Express Pier, follow Wisut Kasat Rd and Wat Indrawihan will be on your left after the junction with Samsen Rd. The reason for Wat Indrawihan's claim to fame is not hard to miss: a 32-metre statue of the Buddha (hence its name in English, the "Temple of the Standing Buddha"). The statue was commissioned in the mid-19th century by Rama IV to house a relic of the Buddha which came from Ceylon (now Sri Lanka). It is not uncommon for such relics as bone and hair fragments to be housed in numerous Buddhist monuments worldwide. While this particular standing Buddha may not be one of the most beautiful, it certainly is impressive. Its enormous toes have become an altar for offerings which usually consist of garlands of fresh flowers. The *bot* contains hundreds of Benjarong funerary urns, as well as traditional-looking but modern murals.

Thewet Flower Market

Retrace your steps back to Samsen Rd, turn right and follow the road until you come to the bridge over Khlong Padung Krung Kasem. There, the Thewet Flower Market will be on your left across the bridge. Flanking both sides of Khlong Phadung Krung Kasem, it runs west from Samsen Road to the Chao Phyra River.

Despite its location in a sedate corner of this quiet backwater of the city, Thewet Flower Market is one of Bangkok's premier plant markets and garden centres. Besides offering a colourful array of flowers and plants from all over the country, the market also stocks an enormous range of gardening goods, including ornamental pots, pond bases and other items. Although Thewet Market is not as extensive as Chatuchak Market, its prices are generally lower, and is a pleasant place to browse because it is not as crowded or busy.

Thewet Flower Market
Opening times: 9:30am to 7:30pm daily
Admission: free

Wat Indrawihan

XCKEN MAY '01

St Francis Xavier Church

Just behind the Thewet Flower Market is the **National Library**. Occupying an extensively planted corner overlooking Samsen and Si Ayutthaya Rds, its exterior incorporates several traditional Thai architectural touches, as do many of the government offices in this part of the city, enlivening otherwise bland modern buildings. The lobby contains a number of paintings by well-known Thai artists, while the library itself contains a large collection of books in both Thai and English. With the National Library on your left, follow Samsen Rd until you come to Soi Samsen 11, which is just past St Gabriel's College, a

St Gabriel's College

BRACKEN JULY '01

Catholic boys' school housed in an attractive three-storey building. Surrounded by mature trees, it would not look out of place in any town in France. Follow the *soi* as it winds its way through a small enclave of Christian churches and schools which runs along the banks of the Chao Phraya River. The St Francis Xavier Church is perhaps the most striking of these buildings, with its portico of three tall arches under a statue of the eponymous saint which faces out over the river near Krung Thon Bridge. It was built in the early 1850s and includes among its congregation a number of Vietnamese Catholics who settled here in the 1930s.

Vimarnmek Palace

Return to Samsen Rd, turn left, and then right at Ratchawithi Rd and follow it until you reach Dusit Park on your right. The Dusit district is perhaps the only part of Bangkok to retain some of the charm and character of the city prior to the rampant development that dominated the second half of the 20th century.

King Rama V and the younger members of the royal family used to cycle along Ratchdamnoen Avenue for exercise and fresh air when official duties at the Grand Palace permitted. Dusit Park, or the Celestial Garden, was built as a New Royal City, connected to the Grand Palace via Ratchdamnoen Avenue, which was intended as a Siamese version of the Champs Elysées. It is still

an oasis of calm today in an otherwise chaotic city. Wide, tree-shaded avenues and *khlongs* are lined with charming Edwardian-era buildings, while the low skyline has been preserved here, adding to the area's charm. Rama V laid out the district along European lines, with grand vistas, broad boulevards, and a practical grid layout for the roads surrounding his new palaces. He was the first Thai king to visit Europe, and came back determined to Westernise his capital. The different palaces, in eclectic mixes of architectural styles, and all set in immaculately maintained gardens, bear testimony to his efforts. Highlights of the park include Vimarnmek Palace, the world's largest golden teak building, and the delightful Abhisek Dusit Throne Hall, which is home to the SUPPORT Museum of traditional arts and crafts.

Other museums in the park include the Royal Carriage Museum, which contains unusual and interesting royal vehicles, including vintage cars and ceremonial carriages, all housed in two long mews buildings. The Old Clock Museum is home to a small collection of antique timepieces from a variety of countries, many of which are wonderfully ornate, but are not always well-

Vimarnmek Palace

Dusit District

119

maintained, or even wound. The Royal Family Museum contains photographs and paintings of members of the ruling Chakri dynasty, past and present. King Bhumibol's Photographic Museum houses photographs taken by the current king, who is a keen amateur photographer. This museum has an added bonus for royal fans because the royal family is featured in many of the photographs.

While the Inner Court of the Grand Palace was said to be haunted, most of the courtiers were comfortable with the ghosts, but this did not apply to the ones at Dusit. There had been a deserted *wat* located here and during the construction of the palace, workmen had dug up large quantities of human bones from its cemetery. The complex is also home to a number of mansions, including the Suan Kulab Palace, a rambling Edwardian-era mansion sitting at the Ai Ayutthaya Rd end of the park. This is not open to public.

Vimarnmek Palace, which means 'Abode in the Clouds', is the world's largest golden teak building. For many years it was nothing but a lone pavilion standing in the middle of its spacious parkland. Separate gardens were laid out for the queen and other members of the royal family, and were named after different patterns of blue-and-white Chinese porcelain, e.g. the Four Seasons, the Lotus, the Swan, etc. The palace itself was constructed entirely without nails, but instead, used wooden pegs to hold the three-storey structure together. Built originally on Kho Si Chang in 1868, it was moved to this site in 1901 where it became the favourite retreat of Rama V and his family, who lived here while waiting for the nearby Chitrlada Palace to be completed. The king was the only adult male allowed to live in the palace, all the other inhabitants were his wives, concubines and children. After it was closed in 1935, it fell into disrepair until Queen Sirikit restored it in time for Bangkok's Bicentennial celebrations in 1982. The guided-tour, which is compulsory if you want to see the interior of the palace, takes in 30 of the 81 rooms via a maze of corridors. Highlights include the audience chambers, the music room, the grand staircases, and the king's apartments, which are contained within an octagonal tower. The rooms are all decorated in early-20th-century Biedermeier style, with European, Siamese, Chinese and even Russian ornaments. The palace was the first building in Thailand to have electricity and an indoor bathroom, and an early light bulb and

Suan Hong Residential hall

Dusit District

Suan Kulab Palace

showerhead are on display. Treasures from the Rattanakosin period include porcelain, furniture, betel-nut sets, the first Thai-alphabet typewriter, state gifts from many foreign countries, hunting trophies and royal photographs. Rama V was known to have a taste for Western design, and this palace, with its verandas and high ceilings, looks more like the extravagant confection of an eccentric Victorian industrialist than a Thai home. There is an elegant little pavilion behind the palace which protrudes into the lake known as the Jade Pool. It affords a pleasant view of the particularly fine cluster of traditional teak houses on the opposite bank which were built so that the king could live in the traditional Thai style whenever he chose. The king had often been received in houses such as this when touring remote provinces and it is said that he had this one built so that when his friends from overseas – he called them his personal friends, his 'phuan ton' – came to see him in Bangkok, he could entertain them in a friendly and less formal atmosphere. These buildings are not open to public.

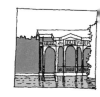

The **SUPPORT Museum** is located in the Abhisek Dusit Throne Hall, which is adjacent to the Vimarnmek Palace gardens and is a showcase for traditional arts and crafts that have been saved from decline by Queen Sirikit, founder of the Promotion of Supplementary Occupations and Related Techniques (SUPPORT). The foundation, built in 1904, is housed in a small, intricately decorated building of wood, brick and stucco, and is somewhat reminiscent of a gingerbread house. Traditional handicrafts on display include nielloware, celadon, lacquerware, and an amazing art form that uses the iridescent green-blue wings of jewel beetles. Some of the designs are created by members of the royal family.

Vimarnmek Palace

Opening times: 9am to 4pm daily, last admission 3:15pm, guided tour compulsory (occasionally closed for state or royal functions)
Admission: B100 (free with Grand Palace ticket within seven days)

SUPPORT Museum

Opening times: 9am to 4pm daily (occasionally closed for state or royal functions)
Admission: Vimarnmek Palace and/or Grand Palace ticket valid

Did You Know?
Queen Saovapha, wife of Rama V, kept the same nocturnal hours as her husband and while she slept during the day, nothing was allowed to disturb the palace's tranquillity. All traffic on the road outside was diverted, and even birds were kept at bay by guards patrolling the grounds armed with silent weapons like blow pipes firing clay bullets.

Ananta Samakorn Throne Hall

Leave the grounds of the Abhisek Dusit Throne Hall by following the signs for the Ananta Samakorn Throne Hall. This vast, ornate, Italianate throne hall was built in 1912, and was home to the Thai parliament for a period of time. It is now used for royal receptions and private functions. It has a spectacular interior but is only open to the public on Children's Day (the second Saturday of January). The throne hall also acts as the focal point at the end of Ratchdamnoen Avenue, which runs here all the way from Sanam Luang. There is an impressive equestrian statue of Rama V at the centre of the parade ground in front of the throne hall. Each year on 23rd October, the anniversary

---

Did You Know?
Rama V introduced chairs into the kingdom: before his reign, Thais sat on the floor, or on floor cushions.

Ananta Samakorn Throne Hall and the King Rama V Equestrian Statue

of the king's death, Thais honour his memory by laying wreaths at the base of the statue. The parade ground is also the site of Thailand's annual Trooping of the Colours ceremony, held in December. The 5th of the month is also the reigning king's birthday, an occasion for which this huge square, along with most of the rest of the city, is lavishly decorated.

Dusit Zoo

Exit the grounds of the Ananta Samakorn Throne Hall via Uthong Nai Rd and Dusit Zoo will be across the road. These lush green grounds were originally the private botanical gardens of Rama V, and some varieties of tropical flora are still cultivated here. It sits at the heart of a green belt which runs from Dusit Park to the Chitrlada Palace. One of Asia's better zoos, it has reasonable space for its birds and the larger mammals that you would expect to find, though like zoos everywhere, some of the enclosures could be bigger. Thanks to its tropical location, Dusit Zoo's elephants are in their native habitat, and they provide rides for visitors. The gardens contain a number of lawns, woods and lakes which are pleasant for strolling through, and there is also a café.

Dusit Zoo
Opening times: 8am to 6pm daily
Admission: B30 (children B5)

Note: White Elephant

The white elephant (*chang samkhan*) holds great importance in Thailand. It is said that Queen Maya became pregnant with the future Buddha after dreaming a white elephant entered her womb. Ever since the 13th century, when King Ramkamhaeng of Sukhothai (now Thailand) gave the animal great prestige, the reigning king's status is reputed to depend on the number of white elephants he owns. Previously a national icon, it was a part of the Siamese flag until 1917. The phrase 'white elephant', which refers to something useless and expensive, hails from the Thai's king's tradition of presenting his enemies with one or more of these beasts as he knew they would become a great drain on resources. White elephants are not necessarily albino, but to qualify for this status the shade of their eyes, trunk, nails, tail, skin, hair and testicles must be as close to white as possible.

Chitrlada Palace

Leaving Dusit Zoo, turn left and follow Uthong Nai Rd until you come to Si Ayutthaya Rd. Turn left again and the grounds of the Chitrlada Palace will be on your left. This is the king's residence and is closed to the public. It was built in the early years of the 20th century and is set in extensive grounds. The palace is hidden from view, but buildings used for agricultural and industrial experiments by the current king, Rama IX, are visible. The royal white elephants are trained and housed on the grounds here. In Bangkok it is really only the few streets around the Chitralada Palace that have remained untouched by the ravages of the second half of the 20th century. With canals on both sides of the roads under the huge shady trees, the visitor can perhaps get a hint of what Sathorn and Wireless Rds must have looked like around 1900.

Wat Benjamabophit

On the right hand side of Si Ayutthaya Rd, before the junction with Rama V Rd, stands the Wat Benjamabophit compound. The temple itself is an extremely successful hybrid of Thai and European architectural elements. It is not old, having been built by Rama V in 1899 to replace two temples which he demolished to make way for the new Dusit palace district. He commissioned his brother, Prince Naris, an architect, who in turn employed Italian architect Hercules Manfredi, to design a new *bot* and cloister for the original Ayutthaya-period temple which stood on the site, and which had been an important shrine. The new *wat* soon became known as the Marble Temple because of the lavish use of Carrera marble to clad its walls. It is featured on the five baht coin.

Elegantly proportioned and laid out in a cruciform style with traditional Thai cascading roofs, the *bot* successfully fuses different traditions with its Victorian-style stained-glass windows depicting scenes from Thai mythology.

Yellow, favoured by the Thais, is the predominant colour used. The temple is well-known for housing one of three sets of beautiful doors inlaid with mother-of-pearl which were salvaged from Wat Borom Buddharam in Ayutthaya. The room housing the ashes of Rama V also contains the revered copy of Phitsanulok's Phra Buddha Chinarat, which is distinguished by a pointed halo. The building, which was Rama V's home when he was a monk, features murals depicting events that occurred during his reign. Arranged around the cloister are 53 different Buddha images, both originals and copies from around Thailand and other Buddhist countries, which the king assembled.

The *wat* is a popular location for witnessing Buddhist monastic rituals, especially the daily alms round. Here, people looking to make merit donate food to the monks who line up along Nakhon Pathom Rd — the exact opposite of the usual practice, where monks go out in search of alms. Located behind the *wat* is a school and numerous other smaller traditional temple buildings lining the canals with their numerous arched bridges, tree-lined walkways and Buddha statues. The entire complex is incredibly serene and is a fitting place to end these walks around the city.

Wat Benjamabophit
Opening times: 7am to 5pm daily
Admission: B20

End of walks.

Wat Benjamabophit

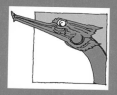

Further Afield

Other places of interest within easy reach of the city centre

Further Afield

This chapter covers individual but isolated architectural gems, such as the Suan Pakkad Palace and The Siam Society compound. It also deals with interesting and historic buildings not covered on the previous walks, such as Wat Arun and the Royal Barge Museum. Included as well is a brief guide to Thailand's most famous bazaar, the Chatuchak Weekend Market.

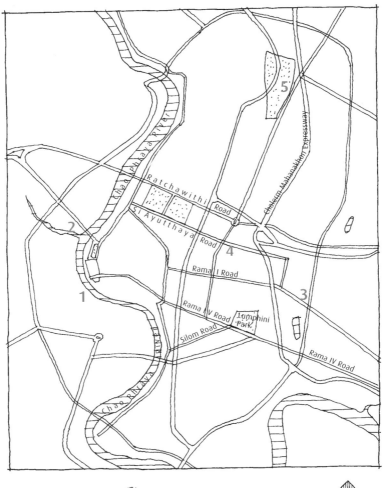

0   5 km

KEY

1. Wat Arun
2. Royal Barge Museum
3. The Siam Society
4. Suan Pakkad Palace
5. Chatuchak Weekend Market

Wat Arun

The nearest Chao Phraya Express Pier to the temple is Thien, where you can hop on a ferry to get across the river. Wat Arun, also known as the Temple of the Dawn, is one of the most striking edifices in Bangkok and an enduring city landmark. It is ancient and has had a number of name changes, being known previously as Wat Makok and Wat Cheng before being named in honour of Aruna, the Indian god of the dawn. It is said that when King Taksin arrived here at sunrise in October 1767 from the sacked capital, Ayutthaya, he decided that this would be the new home of the Emerald Buddha. He then set about enlarging what was quite a small temple into a Royal Chapel.

Rama I and II were mainly responsible for the size of the current temple, while in the 19th century, Rama IV added the ornamentation, which depicts flowers said to evoke the vegetation of Mount Meru, the mythical home of the gods. This decoration, consisting of numerous pieces of broken porcelain donated by local people, is one of the temple's most unusual and attractive features. Up close it looks odd, but from a distance it achieves an eye-catching and colourful effect, especially when seen glittering in the low sunlight of both dawn and dusk.

Seen from the river, as it was ideally meant to be viewed, the temple's striking silhouette is impressive. The monument's style, more akin to Khmer architecture than anything else, is unique in Thailand, and it is this river view that is featured on the ten baht coin, and is also the logo of the Tourism Authority of Thailand.

Wat Arun

The monument's design symbolises Hindu-Buddhist cosmology, with the 67-metre-high central *prang* supposed to represent mythical Mount Meru and its ornamental tiers being worlds within worlds. The layout of the four minor prangs around the central one is a symbolic mandala shape (in Sanskrit the circular figure is seen as a religious symbol of the universe). The circumference of the base is 234 metres, with mondops located at the cardinal points. The rest of the temple complex contains buildings typically found in a *wat*, with the image of the Buddha in the main *bot* sitting above the ashes of devotees. There are a number of Chinese guard figures located at the entrance to the terrace, and these nicely compliment the Chinese-style porcelain decorating the *prangs*.

Wat Arun
Opening times: 7am to 5pm daily
Admission: B20

Did You Know?
This temple was originally known as Wat Cheng, but when King Taksin passed it at dawn one October morning in 1767, and saw how rundown it had become, he vowed to have it restored. It was renamed Wat Arun (Temple of the Dawn) as a result.

BRACKEN AUG '01

Royal Barge Museum

The nearest Chao Phraya Express Pier to this museum is Phra Pinklao. The kingdom's royal barges, a number of which are still used for special occasions such as auspicious royal birthdays, are housed in this warehouse-like structure which became a museum in 1974. Apart from the decorative boats the museum also contains a number of ceremonial objects used in river processions, an exhibition tracing the evolution of these processions, as well as past and present ship-building methods. Most of the boats in the royal collection (of which eight are on display) are reproductions of those built by Rama I. Four others are kept at Wasukree Pier, with 38 more in the Small Boats Section of the Royal Navy. Suphanahong (Golden Swan) is the most important barge in the collection, made during the reign of Rama VI from a single piece of teak more than 50 metres long, it weighs 15 tonnes. Anantanagaraj, bearing a multi-headed *naga* (serpent), is reserved for conveying important Buddha images.

Royal Barge Museum
Opening times: 9am to 5pm daily
Admission: B30 (photography is allowed on payment of a B100 fee)

Note: Royal Transport

The *Khanham* was a covered sedan chair used by the king or females of the royal family, and sometimes also by high-ranking aristocrats during the era of Thailand's absolute monarchy. Sedan chairs, or palanquins, were used for official ceremonies as well as informal visits from the Ayutthaya to the Rattanakosin Periods. There were four different types: the *Yannamat* was used by the king during royal ceremonies, while the roofless *Saliang* served for more general occasions. The *Wo* resembled the *Saliang* except for its canopy and *Khanham*, with its single pole supporting a cradle at its centre, was preferred for long journeys.

Did You Know?
A trip to the Summer Palace at Bang Pa-In was marred by tragedy in 1880 with the drowning of Queen Sunanda. Two or three of the royal barges were involved in a collision but unfortunately, the Queen's was the only one that went down. She was known to be a good swimmer but failed to resurface due to possibly being trapped. It was said that the boatmen didn't dare go to her rescue for fear of touching her, it being against the law to touch royalty. She was only twenty.

Sangaroon House

The Siam Society

Asoke is the nearest Skytrain station. Leave it and follow Sukhumvit Rd, turning left onto Soi Asoke (Soi Sukhumvit 21) and The Siam Society will be on your left. This is a foundation under royal patronage and was established in 1904 to promote the study of Thai history, botany, zoology, anthropology and linguistics. It publishes a scholarly journal containing articles by experts on these subjects, and is also home to an excellent reference library.

The society's headquarters shares its compound with two other interesting buildings. The first, Kamthieng House, was donated to The Siam Society in the 1960s by Khun Kraisri Nimmanahaeminda, a businessman and scholar. It was named in honour of his grandmother, Nang Kamthieng Anusarasundara, who was actually born in the house.

Originally built in Chiang Mai as a traditional Thai country residence, the house was amazingly dismantled there in order to be moved and set up again at its current site. It has since been converted by The Siam Society into an ethnological museum.

Inside, the objects on display give a good idea of what rural life in northern Thailand must have been like in the mid-19th century. The display of farming tools and fish traps on the ground floor illustrates the practical necessity of farmers fishing their flooded paddies to supplement the family's income and diet. Upstairs, the main rooms of the house are much as they would have been when the house was built. The furniture is typically sparse – only a couple of low tables and seating mats arranged across the polished wooden floors, with the obligatory betel nut set at hand. Surplus furniture and utensils are cleverly stored in the rafters. On the lintel above the door to the inner room is a *hum yon*, the carved floral pattern supposedly representing testicles and used to ward off evil spirits. These can still be seen carved or painted over doorways throughout Thailand, even in the most modern of office buildings. The veranda connecting the kitchen to the granary overlooks a garden which has been made to look as authentic as possible and contains a number of areca palm (betel nut) trees.

Nestling close to Kamthieng House in the lush compound is the more recently-acquired Sangaroon House. This traditional Ayutthaya-style house was built in 1988 to house the vast collection of folk craftwork that once belonged to Thai architect Sangaroon Ratagasikorn. Upon his return to Thailand from America (where he had been under the tutelage of Frank Lloyd Wright), Sangaroon began collecting rural utensils after becoming impressed with their efficient design. The result is a fascinating display that includes baskets, fishing pots and takraw balls; all of them simple, functional, elegant – and were even used by Sangaroon as teaching aids!

The Siam Society
Opening times: 9am to 5pm, Tue to Sun
Admission: B100

Suan Pakkad Palace

Alight at Phaya Thai, the nearest Skytrain station, follow Phaya Thai Rd and then turn right onto Si Ayutthaya Rd. On your right will be Suan Pakkad Palace, the former home of Prince and Princess Chumbhot. It consists of a cluster of five traditional teak houses (much like Jim Thompson's house), and was assembled in the 1950s on land that was originally a cabbage patch (*suan pakkad* in Thai, hence its name which is also directly translated in English as Cabbage Patch Palace). A visitor unaware of the site's origins will no doubt find the name rather odd for a building this grand!

Princess Chumbhot was an avid gardener and created the lush landscaped garden we see today. Both she and her husband were also avid art collectors and the palace has been converted into a museum to house their impressive private collections of art and artifacts. Their wide-ranging tastes were manifested in an eclectic selection of objects, from antique lacquered furniture and Khmer sculpture to a selection of traditional Thai musical instruments. There is also an important collection of whorl-patterned red-and-white bronze-age pottery, excavated from tombs at Ban Chiang in Northeast Thailand.

The highlight of any visit to Suan Pakkad Palace has to be its exquisite Lacquer Pavilion, which was built from two temple buildings retrieved by Prince Chumbhot from Ayutthaya province. Immaculately crafted, the pavilion's interior has beautifully detailed black-and-gold lacquered murals depicting scenes from the Buddha's life and the Ramakien. Others show foreigners trading goods, traditional markets, graphic battles, and even some vivid impressions of the Thai version of hell. Equally interesting scenes of ordinary Thai life up to the fall of Ayutthaya in 1767 are among the very few precious murals to survive intact from this period.

Suan Pakkad Palace
Opening times: 9am to 4pm, daily
(guided tours available)
Admission: B100

Suan Pakkad Palace

Further Afield

Chatuchak Weekend Market

If you are walking from the Mo Chit Skytrain station, follow the signs to the market which will be on your right. This extremely popular and very traditional weekend market started life on Sanam Luang where its growth eventually outstripped the available space. In 1982, it moved to Chatuchak Park near the Laadprao intersection where it was initially considered to be too far out of the city. Not anymore. With the stretching of Bangkok's boundaries, the market has now become something of a centre in its own right.

Today, Bangkok's biggest weekend market is said to cover the size of five football fields, and is home to more than 6,000 stalls. A bewildering array of goods is offered, ranging from antiques, discount designer clothes and various specimens of Thai flora, down to exotic animals! (See *Did You Know?*) There is even a hill-tribe section selling artifacts and textiles from all over Thailand and some neighbouring countries. Countless food stalls serve up a huge range of fresh farm produce and seafood that also make for an excellent introduction to the delights of Thai cuisine. Always thronged with bargain hunters, curio seekers and window shoppers alike, the Chatuchak Weekend Market is indeed a very vibrant and buzzing place to spend a weekend afternoon.

Chatuchak Weekend Market
Opening times: 7am to 6pm, Sat and Sun
Admission: free

Did You Know?
Chatuchak Market used to be referred to as the 'wildlife supermarket of the world', due to the number of endangered species being illegally sold here. Fortunately, this particular trade now seems to be in decline.

Chatuchak Weekend Market

Architectural Styles

This chapter explains some of the architectural styles mentioned in the book. Beginning with the different traditional house styles found in various parts of Thailand, it then outlines the five main historic periods of Thai architecture, from Khmer to Rattanakosin. Notes are included on such Western architectural styles as neoclassical and gothic. There is also an overview of the various forms and styles of the different places of worship found in the city, namely Buddhist, Chinese and Indian temples as well as Muslim mosques and Christian churches.

Traditional Thai House

Traditional Thai houses are well adapted to the tropical climate, using natural materials such as hardwoods, bamboo and dried leaves. They are raised on stilts to protect them from flooding during the monsoon season, while steeply slanted roofs deter the build-up of rainwater.

Central Plains House

The Central Plains are the hottest part of the country, and a large veranda that serves as an outside living area is common. Several houses are sometimes clustered around it.

Spirit House

Water House

Houses built on water and along the rivers of the Central Plains are common in flood-prone Bangkok. They are either built on posts above the waterline, or on bamboo rafts which float during floods.

Shophouse

A common building type in Bangkok's Chinatown is the shophouse, which is found similarly throughout the towns and cities of Southeast Asia. The family's living quarters is usually above the level for conducting the business, which can be anything from a small workshop to a restaurant. Usually only two or three storeys in height, the neo-classical style predominates. There are also some handsome art deco examples dating from the 1920s onwards, but in Chinatown, several gothic-style shophouses abound, which is an unusual and rare sight in other cities.

Spirit House

These can be seen everywhere in Bangkok. Usually assembled on poles, spirit houses are built to placate these unseen inhabitants of the land. When you see a patch of virgin forest you can understand the extent of the Thais' reverence for the spirit of so mysterious a place. These little structures are the first thing built when the land is cleared and they are adorned daily with offerings of incense, food and flowers.

Thai Architectural Styles

Khmer
9th to 13th Centuries

Temple complexes, mostly made of stone, were built by the Khmers in Northeast Thailand. A typical construction would be topped by a central *prang* (tower) with the main sanctuary beneath often decorated with reliefs depicting Hindu myth. This prayer area is accessible via a staircase, likely lined with carved *nagas* (serpents). Wat Arun (Temple of the Dawn) on the Chao Phraya River is a Khmer-style temple.

Sukhothai
Mid-13th to 15th Centuries

Thailand's 14th-century capital saw the most radical leap in the country's architecture. King Si Intharathit and his successors built *wihans* and *bots* to house images of the Buddha amid the ruins of earlier Khmer structures. *Chedis*, modelled on the bell-shaped reliquary towers of Ceylon (now Sri Lanka), were also often added. The Sukhothai Hotel on Sathorn Rd borrows elegantly from this architectural tradition.

Ayutthaya
Mid-14th to 18th Centuries

Little of the architecture of Ayutthaya survived the destruction of the Burmese invasion of 1767, but the style seems to have been a subtle modification of Khmer *prangs* and Ceylon-style *chedis*, with elaborate decoration of *cho fas* (the decorative pieces on top of the roof that resemble the mystical *garuda* bird) and door and window pediments. Wat Ratchaburana in Chinatown has an Ayutthaya-style *prang*.

Lanna
Mid-13th to 19th Centuries

The religious buildings from this period took their influence from Sukhothai, India and Ceylon. Although few buildings remain from Lanna's golden age of the 14th and 15th centuries, later temples, in places like Chiang Mai, often featured the intricate woodcarving and gilded *cho fas* and murals associated with this style. The small Wat Muang Kae on Charoen Krung Soi 34 has many Lanna-style decorative timber features.

Lanna style (Wat Muang Kae)

Rattanakosin style (arch, Grand Palace)

Rattanakosin
Late 18th Century to present day

Also known as the Bangkok style, the first *wihans* and *bots* built in the new capital after the fall of Auytthaya were similar to the ones that had been destroyed by the Burmese. Later, larger and more elaborate temples were built, and by the end of the 19th century, such buildings as Wat Benjamabophit (Marble Temple) increasingly borrowed from the West, as did many others in the Grand Palace complex. The balcony in the Grand Palace complex overlooking Sanam Chai Rd, from which the king would appear to his people, is typically Rattanakosin in style with its mix of Thai and Western elements.

Western Architectural Styles
Neoclassical

Shiny new skyscrapers and the endless vistas of dusty concrete apartment blocks may lend a somewhat Western flavour to downtown Bangkok, but the elegance of the West's architectural expression is lost on the majority. Thankfully, there are some rather more attractive exceptions in the city. These invariably fall into one of two styles: neoclassical or gothic. Neoclassicism was a throwback to ancient Greece and Rome, from the time before and shortly after the birth of Christ. The era had a style that was elegant and harmonious but it disappeared with the fall of the Roman Empire. It was revived in the 17th century, first in Italy and then throughout the rest of Europe and North America, by Andrea Palladio, an Italian architect who studied the ruins of ancient Rome and adapted their styles to suit his era. With the spread of the European empires, this style became global.

Gothic

This style developed in Northern Europe in the 12th century. Its main characteristic was the pointed arch. The gothic style had died out by the time of the Renaissance but experienced a revival from the mid-18th century, partly as a reaction to the centuries of neoclassicism, and also due to the huge popularity of gothic novels at the time. Thus began the battle for supremacy between both styles that raged in the 19th century across Europe and even in Asia. Still, the gothic never really caught on in a big way in Bangkok, with the exception of Christian churches and some of the shophouses of Chinatown.

Places of Worship
Thai Temples

The tolerant nature of the Thai people mean that there are very many places of worship in the city belonging to other faiths. Thai Buddhist temples dominate, however, and are built along guidelines that have changed little over the centuries. Invariably they are elaborately decorated, but also have a very practical function as a community centre of sorts, particularly in rural areas. Rarely is there a temple without a monastery attached to it for the resident monks or nuns. Laid out with particular care paid to religious symbolism, a Buddhist temple features several typical elements. The bodhi tree – beneath where the Buddha supposedly sat while attaining Enlightenment – is usually found only in larger temples. The *bot* is an ordination hall, usually reserved for monks, which faces East and often houses the temple's most important image of the Buddha. A *chedi* is a solid structure, usually bell-shaped, encasing a relic of the Buddha or the ashes of a king. Usually, a number of temples were specifically built around a *chedi* due to its sacred purpose. The cloister encloses the main part of the temple and its walls are often decorated with murals. The more important temples will house statues of the Buddha in rows, while the larger temples will have a library of sacred texts, and they are housed in a building known as the *ho tri*. A *mondop* is a square-based structure that usually contains an object of veneration and topped with a spire. The *wihan* is an assembly hall, similar to the *bot*, but usually larger and accessible by the laity. There may be more than one of them in a temple complex.

Thai temple (stupa, Grand Palace)

Chinese temple (Da Ben Tou Gong Temple, Songwat Rd)

Chinese Temples

The form of the traditional Chinese temple is usually based on that of the traditional Chinese house, consisting of a group of pavilions ranged around open courtyards. They are also usually built in strict accordance with *feng shui* precepts in an attempt to achieve a balance between the temple's *yin* and *yang* elements. Location also plays an important part in the decision to construct a Chinese temple; for example, being close to water will result in favourable *feng shui*. Chinese temples can be dedicated either to one specific deity or to more than one god. In fact, some are even syncretic in nature, which means that various Chinese faiths (Buddhist, Taoist, Confucian, etc.,) are welcome to worship there. The temple's layout, with its sequence of courtyards and worship halls, is often on axial lines and reflects the Confucian virtue of *li* (the manner of humbling oneself in deference to others). They are invariably rich in gilt-covered decorative carvings, mouldings and murals, often with the dragon as a prominent decorative feature.

Indian Temples

Bangkok has a number of important Hindu temples dotted throughout its centre. Elaborately sculpted, they stand out even in this already garish city in all their Technicolor glory. Always square-shaped in plan (Hindus regard the square as the perfect shape), a complex set of rules governs the siting, design and building of every temple. These rules are based on numerology, astronomy, astrology and religious law, and are so complicated that it is customary for each

Indian temple
(Sri Mahamariamman
Temple, Silom Rd)

temple to keep its own specific set of data, almost as if they were religious texts. Each temple is dedicated to a particular god. Temples are a constant hub of activity and a focal point for the Hindu community which gathers to celebrate many different rites and festivals. Many Thais also worship in Hindu temples as Buddhism sprang directly from Hinduism itself (and the Buddha was also born in Lumbini, which is in India). When visiting a Hindu temple, remember to dress conservatively and to remove your shoes before entering.

Muslim Mosques

Arabs from the Middle East traded in Siam (now Thailand) centuries before Bangkok was founded. Thailand's immediate neighbours to the south, Malaysia and Indonesia, are predominantly Muslim countries. A large proportion of the population in southern Thailand is also Muslim, and there are significant pockets of Islamic faith dotted around the capital. The mosques in Bangkok are traditional in form and layout, and often serve as respective centres for Islamic studies. While they are not as grand or imposing as those typically built by Thailand's Muslim neighbours, they often have more charm and character as a result. Besides the customary dome, there is often only one minaret from which the muezzin calls the faithful to prayer (though the human voice has increasingly been replaced in most mosques by recordings broadcast via loudspeakers). When entering a mosque remember that shoes must be left outside, and people, especially women, must be dressed appropriately, i.e. no shorts or singlets.

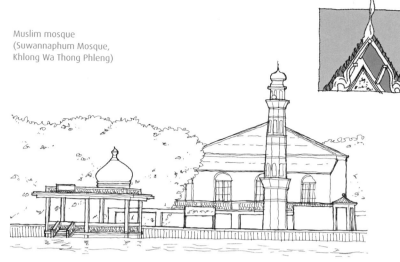

Muslim mosque
(Suwannaphum Mosque,
Khlong Wa Thong Phleng)

Christian Churches

Bangkok has a fair number of Christian places of worship. Both Roman Catholic and Protestant churches tend to have a standard cross-shaped layout (with the former usually being more decorative). The collapse of the Roman Empire around the 5th century CE had people converting to Christianity in increasingly larger numbers. To accommodate the crowds, marketplaces known as *basilicas* became used as places of worship. For the next few hundred years, Christian churches tended to follow this form, and were built in heavy, square-shaped fashion. After 800 CE, Western-European Christians became galvanised with the establishment of the Holy Roman Empire under Charlemagne. This new spirit of identity was reflected in their buildings. Advances in building technology also allowed for a new lightness of construction and an airy brightness to enter churches for the first time. This new style became known as the gothic, and it was also about this time that the plan of the church finally took on the recognisable cross-shape seen today. Although other shapes and forms were experimented with in Rome and other Western cities during the Renaissance, the cross-shape has consistently remained the most popular.

Christian church
(Kalawar Church,
Thanon Yotha)

GLOSSARY

Avatar   earthly manifestation of a deity

Bai sema   boundary stone to mark consecrated ground

Ban   house or village

Benjarong   Polychromatic ceramics made in China for the Thai market, (lit. five colours)

Bodhisattva   in Mahayana Buddhism, an enlightened being

Bot   main sanctuary in a temple

Brahma   one of the Hindu Trinity: the Creator

Chedi   reliquary tower in Buddhist temple

Dharma   the teachings or doctrine of the Buddha

Dharamchakra   Buddhist Wheel of Law

Erawan   mythical three-headed elephant: Indra's vehicle

Farang   foreign, Western, a foreigner from the West

Ganesh   Hindu elephant-headed deity

Garuda   mythical Hindu creature: half-man, half-bird: Vishnu's vehicle

Hanuman   Monkey god

Indra   Hindu king of the gods

Jataka   stories of the 500 hundred lives of the Buddha

Khlong   canal

Khon   classical dance-drama

Khun   Mr, Mrs, Ms

Kinnari   mythical creature: half-woman, half-bird

Lakhon   classical dance-drama

Lak muang   city pillar, revered home for the city's guardian spirit

Meru   mythical mountain home of the gods in Hindu and Buddhist cosmologies

Mondop   small, square temple building to house minor images

Muay Thai   Thai boxing

Naga	mythical dragon-headed serpent in Buddhism and Hinduism
Nirvana	final liberation from the cycle of rebirths, state of non-being
Prang	central tower in a Khmer temple
Rama	king of the Chakri dynasty. Human manifestation of Hindu deity Vishnu
Ramayana	Hindu epic of good versus evil
Romanesque	architectural style in Europe from the 7th to the 12th centuries characterised by round-arched openings and heavy stone carving
Sanskrit	sacred language of Hinduism, also used in Buddhism
Shiva	one of the Hindu Trinity: the Destroyer
Soi	lane
Songkhran	Thai New Year (in April)
Takraw	game played with a rattan ball
Tha	pier
Thanon	road
Theravada	main school of Buddhist faith in Thailand
Tripitaka	Buddhist scriptures
Uma	Shiva's consort
Vishnu	one of the Hindu Trinity: the Preserver
Wai	Thai gesture of greeting and thanks
Wat	temple
Wihan	temple assembly hall for the laity

Glossary

A Note on Language

Whereas most Thais who are used to dealing with foreigners speak some English, you'll delight them if you at least try to make the effort to speak a few words. Thai is a tonal language with five different tones: low, middle, high, rising and falling; this means that the same word can have up to five different meanings depending on the tone used.

Thai is also very monosyllabic and staccato-sounding, so if you're a Westerner you'll have to suppress the urge to infuse emotion into what you're saying in Thai, it will only confuse matters.

You should also try to end your sentences with the word *'krap'* if you're a male and *'kaa'* if you're a female as it's considered polite. Don't let laughter at your efforts to speak the language put you off, amusement is often nothing more than the Thai way of showing their appreciation for your efforts.

Street signs in Bangkok are almost always written in Roman script as well as Thai, but the English translations can be very inconsistent, so be careful if you need to ask for directions, what you read may not be the actual pronunciation in Thai.

Some Useful Thai

Conversation

Hello	*sa wah dee*
How are you?	*pen yan gai?*
I'm fine	*sa bai dee*
Do you speak English?	*poot angrit?*
I can't speak Thai	*poot thai mai dai*
I don't know	*mai roo*
I understand	*kao jai*
I don't understand	*mai kao jai*
It doesn't matter	*mai pen rai*
Yes	*chai* or **krap** (male) **kaa** (female)
No	*mai chai*
Please	*kor*
Thank you	*kap khun*
No, thank you	*mai aow kap khun*
Sorry	*kor towt*

Directions

Here	*tee nee*
There	*tee nun*
What?	*a rai?*
Why?	*tum mai?*
Where?	*tee nai?*
How?	*yang rai?*
How far?	*kiai tao rai?*
How long?	*nan tao rai?*
How much?	*tao rai?*
Good	*dee*
Bad	*mai dee*
Open	*bpert*
Closed	*bpit*
Left	*sai*
Right	*kwah*
Straight on	*yoo drong nah*
Between	*ra wahng*
On the corner of	*drong hooa moom*
Near	*glai* (falling tone)
Far	*glai* (mid tone)
Up	*keun*
Down	*long*
Entrance	*tahng kao*
Exit	*tahng ork*
Ticket	*tua*
Free	*free* (i.e. no charge)
Toilet	*horng nahm*
Temple	*wat*
Market	*ta lat*
Museum	*pi pit ta pun*
Palace	*wang*
Park	*suan*
Road	*ta non*
Lane	*soi*
River	*meh nam*
Canal	*khlong*
Bridge	*sap han*
Boat	*ria*
Ferry	*ria doi sam*
Pier	*ta*
Train	*rot fai*
Taxi	*tak si*

Numbers

0	*soon*
1	*neung*
2	*song*
3	*sahm*
4	*see*
5	*hah*
6	*hok*
7	*jet*
8	*bpairt*
9	*gao*
10	*sip*
11	*sip et*
12	*sip song*
13	*sip sahm*
14	*sip see*
15	*sip hah*
16	*sip hok*
17	*sip jet*
18	*sip bpairt*
19	*sip gao*
20	*yee sip*
21	*yee sip et*
22	*yee sip song*
30	*sahm sip*
40	*see sip*
50	*hah sip*
60	*hok sip*
70	*jet sip*
80	*bpairt sip*
90	*jao sip*
100	*neung roi*
101	*roi et*
200	*song roi*
1,000	*neung pun*

Glossary

LISTINGS

GENERAL
Skytrain operation hours: 6am to midnight

Bangkok telephone directory enquiries: 1133

www.siam.net/guide
Siam Net, tourist information

www.tat.or.th
Tourism Authority of Thailand (TAT), tourist information

www.ethailand.com
phone numbers and information for Bangkok and Thailand

www.bangkokpost.net/realtime/whatson.html
daily English-language newspaper

www.nationmulitmedia.com
daily English-language newspaper

www.bkkmetro.com
monthly English-language listings magazine

www.siam-society.org
lists upcoming study trips to historic places of interest and lectures

www.bangkoksports.com
lists athletic options including Aussie rules football, extreme sports, biking clubs, horse riding, ice skating, polo and running

www.buddhanet.net
lists temples throughout the country

WALKS
PRATUNAM
Jim Thompson's House
www.jimthompsonhouse.org

Siam Ocean World
www.siamoceanworld.com

Baiyoke Sky Hotel
Tel: 656 3000
www.baiyokehotel.com

WIRELESS ROAD
Swissôtel Nai Lert Park
Tel: 253 0123
www.nailertpark.swissotel.com

British Embassy
Tel: 305 8333

Royal Netherlands Embassy
Tel: 309 5200

US Embassy
Tel: 205 4000

SILOM ROAD
Sukhothai Hotel
Tel: 287 0222
www.sukhothai.com

Westin Banyan Tree Hotel
Tel: 679 1200
www.westin-bangkok.com

Metropolitan Hotel
Tel: 625 3333
www.metropolitan.como.bz

Jim Thompson's Thai Silk Company
www.jimthompson.com

Snake Farm
Tel: 252 0161-4
www.redcross.or.thai

Neilson-Hays Library
www.neilsonhayslibrary.com

Silom Village Trade Centre
www.silomvillage.co.th

CHAROEN KRUNG ROAD
Oriental Hotel
Tel: 659 9000
www.mandarinoriental.com

French Embassy
Tel: 266 8250-6

Portuguese Chancellery
Tel: 234 7435

Royal Orchid Sheraton Hotel
Tel: 266 0123
www.starwoodhotels.com/
sheraton

RATTANAKOSIN
Wat Pho
www.watpho.com

Institute of Massage
Tel: 221 3686
www.watphomassage.com

Grand Palace
www.palaces.thai.net

National Museum
Tel: 224 1333
www.thailandmuseum.com

National Theatre (box office)
Tel: 224 1342, 221 0171

National Gallery
Tel: 282 2639-40
www.thailandmuseum.com

BANG LAMPHOO
Corrections Museum, Romanareerat Park
www.correct.go.th

DUSIT DISTRICT
Vimarnmek Palace
Tel: 280 5926, 281 1569
www.palaces.thai.net

SUPPORT Museum
www.thailandmuseum.com

FURTHER AFIELD
Wat Arun
www.watarun.org

Royal Barge Museum
www.thailandmuseum.com

The Siam Society
www.siam-society.org

Suan Pakkad Palace
www.suanpakkad.com

LIST OF ILLUSTRATIONS

List of Illustrations

LIST OF MAPS

LIST OF ICONS

Must See
Pages: 18, 24, 26, 37, 46, 57, 71, 82, 87, 94, 100, 106, 109, 118, 125, 130, 134, 136.

National Monument
Pages: 18, 22, 23, 44, 49, 51, 52, 56, 57, 58, 61, 68, 74, 82, 84, 86, 87, 94, 102, 104, 106, 107, 118, 123, 125, 130, 133, 134.

Good View
Pages: 26, 42, 90, 106.

See At Night
Pages: 46, 47, 51, 71, 109, 110.

Drinking
Pages: 21, 32, 42, 46, 47, 52, 57, 71, 109, 110.

Eating
Pages: 21, 26, 32, 42, 47, 52, 57, 71, 109, 110, 124, 136.

Shopping
Pages: 18, 21, 44, 46, 47, 52, 56, 57, 71, 72, 74, 76, 78, 92, 109, 115, 136.

Lists Of Maps & Icons

INDEX

Index

Index

NOTES